Young people's life and schooling in rural areas

the Tufnell Press,
London,
United Kingdom
www.tufnellpress.co.uk
email contact@tufnellpress.co.uk

British Library Cataloguing-in-Publication Data
A catalogue record for this book is
available from the British Library
paperback ISBN   *1872767745*
ISBN-13   *978-1-872767-74-1*

Kindle

Copyright © 2019 Elisabet Öhrn and Dennis Beach
The moral rights of the authors have been asserted.
Database rights the Tufnell Press (maker).

All rights reserved. No part of this publication may be reproduced, stored in a retrieval system, or transmitted in any form or by any means, electronic, mechanical, photocopying, recording or otherwise, without the prior permission of the publisher, or expressly by law, or under terms agreed with the appropriate reprographic rights organisation.

Young people's life and schooling in rural areas

edited by
Elisabet Öhrn and Dennis Beach

The Ethnography and Education book series aims to publish a range of authored and edited collections including both substantive research projects and methodological texts and in particular we hope to include recent PhDs. Our priority is for ethnographies that prioritise the experiences and perspectives of those involved and that also reflect a sociological perspective with international significance. We are particularly interested in those ethnographies that explicate and challenge the effects of educational policies and practices and interrogate and develop theories about educational structures, policies and experiences. We value ethnographic methodology that involves long-term engagement with those studied in order to understand their cultures, that use multiple methods of generating data and that recognise the centrality of the researcher in the research process.

www.ethnographyandeducation.org

The editors welcome substantive proposals that seek to:

> explicate and challenge the effects of educational policies and practices and
> interrogate and develop theories about educational structures, policies and experiences,
> highlight the agency of educational actors,
> provide accounts of how the everyday practices of those engaged in education and instrumental in social reproduction.

The editors are

> Professor Dennis Beach, University College of Borås, Sweden,
> Professor Sofia Marques da Silva, Porto University, Portuagal,
> Professor Geoff Troman, Roehampton University, London and
> Professor Geoffrey Walford, University of Oxford.

Details of recent titles in this series can be found at the end of this book

Contents

Chapter 1
   Introduction
      Dennis Beach and Elisabet Öhrn   1

Chapter 2
   Young people talk about their 'rural' place: A rural idyll?
      Per-Åke Rosvall and Maria Rönnlund   22

Chapter 3
   'The local place' in the pedagogic practices
      Per-Åke Rosvall   45

Chapter 4
   Careers, agency and place. Rural students reflect on their future
      Maria Rönnlund   65

Chapter 5
   Places and schools in times of demographic change
      Monica Johansson   83

Chapter 6
   Reproduction of social relations in rural schools and communities
      Maria Rönnlund and Per-Åke Rosvall   104

Chapter 7
   Education politics and rural secondary schools
      Dennis Beach and Monica Johansson   121

Chapter 8
   Closing discussion
      Dennis Beach and Elisabet Öhrn   139

Ethnography and Education publications   154

Chapter 1

Introduction

Dennis Beach and Elisabet Öhrn

Metrocentricity and neglect of the rural in educational research

A key motivation for the research presented in this book is that urban studies dominate contemporary educational research (e.g. Hargreaves, Kvalsund and Galton, 2009). Consequently, knowledge of young people's marginalisation and participation in education and wider society is based on observations of life in limited geographical/social contexts. The predominant metrocentricity leads to the neglect of needs that are not present, or readily apparent, in cities (Farrugia, 2014) and underestimation of problems faced by rural youth. This is despite findings that it is mainly young people from outside metropolitan regions who express a lack of involvement in Swedish society and a dearth of confidence in both government and parliament (e.g. Swedish National Board for Youth Affairs, 2010). Thus, to obtain a more representative picture of young people's situations and education we need to explore rural youths and their schooling more broadly and deeply.

The development of different communities and regions within a country might vary quite markedly. In Sweden, populations and wealth are still generally growing in cities, while rural populations are shrinking, and with some exceptions they are becoming more impoverished. Almost half of the country's rural municipalities have smaller populations today than three decades ago, schools are closing and students have to travel further to get their education, often at greater cost than before and with sparser state subsidies to support them (Fjellman, Yang Hansen and Beach, 2018).

The differences between areas of urban development and rural decline begs questions about the claimed aspects of justice and equity in the Swedish education system. Admittedly, this system seems to be ostensibly open and inclusive (Gudmundsson, 2013). Currently, for example, in Swedish schools more than eighty-five per cent of all child cohorts between the ages of three and nineteen are included for at least six hours each weekday (outside vacations) in some form of organised institutional education or day-care. This is regardless of their social class, gender, racial or ethnic heritage or any possible physical or mental disabilities (Beach and Dyson, 2016; Beach, 2018). However, inequalities still loom large, and as noted by various authors (e.g. Åberg-Bengtsson, 2009; Beach, From, Johansson and Öhrn, 2018; Beach, Johansson, Öhrn, Rönnlund and Rosvall, 2018; Fjellman et al.); rural-urban disparities have long blemished the social democratic welfare state's record, and recently seem to have significantly expanded.

Research about education, place and the marginalisation of young people

The presence of studies on young people and their education in marginalised urban areas, stands in sharp contrast to the relative silence from research about rural youth and education. A Swedish review of thirty years of research on small rural schools concludes that there are few studies, and furthermore that the existing ones are primarily about the quality of educations, students' academic performances or the closing down of schools (Åberg-Bengtsson, 2009). Studies of schools in their contexts — that are more frequent in urban research — are deemed very rare. That goes for the Nordic countries in general but it is said to be particularly obvious in Sweden where such research is 'almost non-existent' (Hargreaves et al., 2009, p. 28). This silence on the rural is not restricted to educational research, but applies to other fields as well. For instance, youth research is said to seldom target rural youth and existing studies to focus on 'move or stay'-issues (Svensson 2010, p. 279; also Möller, 2011; Waara, 2011).

Core elements of the rather rich literature on urban education and place are the urban contrasts: the associations of urban areas with poverty, marginalisation and problems together with contrasting opportunities, high culture and capital (Öhrn and Weiner, 2007). Corresponding physical segregation has also been highlighted, with people of low income/education being grouped together in certain areas while those with more capital live elsewhere. The former groups are subjected to territorial stigmatisation (Wacquant, 2007, p. 68) and people living in stigmatised areas are 'clearly aware of these pathologising discourses' (Archer, Hollingworth and Mendick, 2010, p. 32). Such discourses appear to be widespread across nations. For instance, there are obvious resemblances in expressions of marginalised urban youth in Sweden talking about their neighbourhoods as *poor*, *immigrant* and *ghetto* areas (Öhrn, 2011), with those of urban Canadian students who refer to their schools as *ghetto* or *slum* schools for poor kids (Kennelly and Dillabough, 2008, p. 499). Thus, place and location are strong signifiers of identity, class and ethnicity, and communicate expectations of those living in marginalised urban places (e.g. Andersson, 2003; Gietz-Johansen, 2003).

In urban areas, social differences and conflicts are visible through housing and school segregation: *we* and the *others* are literally and visibly separated. Whether (and if so how) place signifies social positions in rural areas, with its less distinct housing segregation, is not clear. Some studies suggest that more complex relations may be manifested in heterogenous social groupings than in homogenous ones, where students' categorisation of *the others* may be less ambiguous (Lindbäck and Sernhede, 2010). It has also been claimed that class and ethnicity may be more central categorisations for youth in metropolitan schools than in rural schools (Öhrn, 2012a), and that other kinds of social factors, such as family background, may be more important than class for social positioning in rural areas (Holm, 2008). However, the roles and impact of class in such respects have received less attention in rural settings than in urban ones, so its importance is still debatable.

There are different views on whether there is more social cohesion in rural communities (Solstad, 2009). Some would argue that small communities are *closer*, with more social fellowship building on common history and experiences, and family relationships. In contrast, others hold that rural communities do not necessarily have more in common or a greater fellowship than other areas. Urban researchers have proposed that metropolitan areas are becoming more fragmented and losing their former *community spirit* (Sernhede, 2007, p. 466; Wacquant, 2007), but questions about the strength of local fellowship in rural areas have also been raised (Heggen, Myklebust and Øia, 2001). Thus, there are clear needs for analyses of urban-rural relations and whether social fragmentation is a generic trend in contemporary Western societies, its variations, and its implications for young people's belonging and sense of participation.

Research about education, local relations and young people's participation

Media and policy debates have typically depicted young people's exclusion and resistance as urban (principally male) issues (e.g. Nolan and Anyon, 2004; Öhrn, 2012b). Ruralities are often presented as more idyllic, with less prevalence of social problems and challenges than urban areas. More concern and anxiety are expressed for urban youth, although Swedish media has recently paid attention to nationalist and xenophobic sympathies in rural areas. For example, the greater support for the nationalist Sweden Democrats in rural than in metropolitan areas has been highlighted (Novus/Svt, 2018[1]).

Urban research suggests that schools in marginalised areas generally provide little help for young people to understand such social conditions and trends, let alone to develop a critical perception of their social position and challenge it (Beach and Sernhede, 2011; Schwartz and Öhrn, 2012). Whether schools in rural areas differ in this respect largely remains to be seen. According to previous reviews this is not a focus of Swedish rural research (Åberg-Bengtsson, 2009). Occasional studies point to a more open attitude towards the local community in rural schools (Marklund, 2000), and for the rural curriculum to include activities and competences relevant to local businesses, such as hunting, fishing and forestry (Gustafsson and Öhrn, 2012). Similarly, Eskilsson (2010) found that students of Swedish rural schools are often allowed leave of absence to participate in such activities. However, knowledge of these and associated phenomena is scarce. Thus, as noted for instance by Hargreaves et al.,(2009), there is a need for more research to understand how local conditions and community are addressed in rural education, and the implications for young people's future work and life in rural communities. Rural schools may conceivably be more likely to address their local conditions in teaching, as doing so may seem less potentially dangerous than in some urban areas with high tensions. However, some rural areas also face challenging conditions, including depopulation, high unemployment, poverty, shortages of teachers and schools, and poor future prospects.

The project

Against this background, we designed a project on *Rural youth—education, place and participation* (VR 2013-2142, funded by the Swedish Research Council from 2014 to 2017). The project was planned with the aim of developing a deeper understanding of rural youth's education, their participation and agency. It set out to research young people's social inclusion and participation in rural schools and how schools in different rural areas address young people's opportunities to work and social inclusion. Central to this, and explored by use of ethnographic methods, are youth's understandings of belonging, social relationships, differences and conflicts in various places, and the ways these are addressed (or not) in teaching to allow for young people to understand and act on their social position.

---

1. www.svt.se/special/valjarbarometern, retrieved 2018-03-08

From idea to practice and from ethnography to multi-sited ethnography

Ethnography can be straightforwardly described as participant observation. However, as noted by Walford (2018), a complicating factor is that use of the term has broadened in recent decades and for some it has now become almost synonymous with qualitative research. The association with qualitative research misrepresents ethnography, and has not been traditionally recognised by ethnographic researchers, who often generate quantitative data as well as field-notes and descriptions to support their arguments.

As with Walford, we have not drawn any hard lines between qualitative and quantitative methods and their data types. Rather, as suggested by Hammersley and Atkinson (1983), we have aimed to produce multiple types of data in our investigations in attempts to foster robust understanding of the researched settings and to interrogate, challenge and develop relevant theoretical ideas. Thus, although we have not included sophisticated statistical analyses in the research and tended to rely on non-numerical forms of data, we recognise that quantitative analysis can play valuable roles in ethnographic research (notably for characterising and assessing effects of socio-economic and demographic factors). This is consistent with descriptions by Walford (2018) and Troman (2006) of ethnography as a practice involving seven key principles:

- A focus on the study of cultural formation and maintenance;
- The use of multiple methods and the generation of rich, diverse forms of data;
- The direct involvement and long-term engagement of the researcher(s);
- A recognition that the researcher is the main research instrument;
- High valuation of accounts of participants' perspectives and understandings;
- Engagement in a spiral of data production, hypothesis building and theory testing—leading to further data production; and
- A focus on a particular case in depth, but providing the basis for theoretical generalisation (see also Troman, 2006, p. 1).

Our original project idea set out to enact and operationalise these seven principles in six separate and particularly selected schools in different rural places through long-term participant observation and direct involvement and sustained researcher engagement at each setting. This was done to provide detailed accounts and thick descriptions of how the everyday practices of those engaged in educational processes took place and how these events were implicated in broader social relations and cultural production. The agency of educational subjects in these processes at each site was also going to be given specific attention in this analysis. However, when enacting the project a number of challenges had to be confronted and these resulted in innovatory grafts of some significant importance.

One of these grafts was introduced early, already at the stage of formulating the project plan. It concerned the diversity of rurality *per se* and quite simply that there are many different forms of rurality so that in order to avoid stereotyping rurality as one category, we had to include different types of rural areas in our investigations, such as sparsely populated areas, tourist municipalities and small industrial (and 'de-industrialised') communities. These each represent an official category in definitions of rural places (SKL, 2011) and the schools selected for the study were chosen to provide a variation along these lines. The one tourist municipality in the study however, was found to also be able to categorise as sparsely populated, and in the book we mainly discuss along this devide of sparsely populated and de/industrialised rural communities. The characteristics of the schools and their municipalities are summarised in Table 1. All but two of them were the only secondary schools in their respective municipalities.

Table 1. Researched schools and their locations *

Areas/ Schools	Catchment/ less or more than 3000	Upper secondary school in the municipality or distance to	Distance to higher education facility	History of production **	Current labour market
Coastal school/ De/industrialised	More than 3000	No, between 50 and 100 km to nearest, a wide range of national and local programmes	Between 50 and 100 km	Primary sector	Secondary and tertiary sectors
Inland school/ Sparse	Less than 3000	No, between 50 and 100 km to nearest, only a few of the national programmes	Between 150 and 200 km	Primary sector	Primary and secondary sectors

Areas/ Schools	Catchment/ less or more than 3000	Upper secondary school in the municipality or distance to	Distance to higher education facility	History of production **	Current labour market
Mountain school Tourist/ Sparse	Less than 3000	Yes, only a few of the national programmes	More than 300 km	Primary sector	Tertiary sector
River School/ De/industrialised	More than 3000	Yes, most of the national programmes	Between 100 and 150 km	Military base, secondary sector	Secondary and tertiary sectors
Forest school/ Sparse	Less than 3000	Yes, only a few of the national programmes	Between 150 and 200 km	Primary sector	Primary and secondary sectors
Sea school De/industrialised	More than 3000	No, app. 50 km to nearest	Between 100 and 150 km	Primary and secondary	Secondary sector

* A similar table but with three types of areas (urban, peri-urban and sparse) rather than the two shown here (de/industrialised and sparse) appears in some previous publications based on the project (e.g. Beach et al., 2018).

** The primary, secondary and tertiary sectors represent various business types and the goods they produce and sell. However, they may be considered links in a production chain, from extraction of raw materials (primary) through manufacture (secondary) to servicing end consumers (tertiary).

As indicated by names of the schools, the selected rural areas include both inland, mountainous and/or forested areas and seaside/coastal areas. They are located in both southern and northern Sweden. As the third largest country by area in the European Union,[2] but only tenth biggest in terms of population, Sweden is sparsely populated. The most sparsely populated areas are mainly in the North, although there are also some further South. These areas are generally associated with forestry, timber, wood-pulp production, tourism, and previously in some cases mining.

2. europa.eu/european-union/about-eu/figures/living_en

Contextual constraints in our ethnography and multi-sited ethnography

Although we would have liked to spend more time in the field at each site, due to the restricted budgets granted by our main funding agency, a maximum of five weeks of continuous fieldwork was considered possible in each school for each of the three project's field researchers. The plan was to carry out this fieldwork in 2015-2016 at each site, and follow up this restricted but sustained period of participant observation with further occasional visits. Temporally compressing fieldwork in this way is one of several ways of using research time ethnographically (Jeffrey and Troman, 2004). However, other demands on the field research team's time prohibited accommodation of five consecutive weeks in the field at each site, and corresponding time had to be divided into 1-2 week visits at each site by each field researcher followed up (at one site) by occasional visits.

Jeffrey and Troman (2004) call this kind of temporal ordering of fieldwork an intermittent time mode. As an ideal type it is meant to allow a flexible approach to the frequency of site visits and is organised around the concept of progressive focusing in ethnography in relation to the development and continual evaluation of a characteristic ethnographic spiral of research planning and reflection. Data production and analysis, new planning, and further data production and analysis are organised in an ongoing dialectic process.

However, instead of this flexible approach to fieldwork as an evolving process, we had to adopt the intermittent time mode *a priori*, which curtailed researcher autonomy. We did so though within a collective approach to the ethnography, where although each individual field researcher concentrated primarily on one designated research site, data and ideas were collectively shared, and investigations were also strongly jointly planned through regular collective discussions. The collectivisation of the ethnographic venture involved the team members doing the following:

- Reading and contributing to a collective and continually evolving joint plan of action that maintained a common focus but also sufficient degrees of freedom for individual variations in terms of project activities where this was jointly considered to be of value to the project aims
- Reading each individual researcher's fieldwork narratives carefully to identify the main concepts and ideas, their possible relationships and general implications
- Checking the relevance of the concepts within the scope of the project
- Identifying patterns in the field terms of the cultural processes that may be evident.

Thus, our collective ethnography contained elements that are common in multi-sited ethnography and vertical case analysis, where joint discussions and analyses are often used in such a manner. This is due to their recognised ability to facilitate identification of tentative themes and questions about emergent ideas and development of common practices, discourses and tools to keep the research productive and flexibly focused across different institutional arrangements and various sites over time (Eisenhart, 2017). To a large degree we developed multi-sitedness and cooperation partly as a way to cope with contingent developments and emerging needs. As a more deliberately planned activity Eisenhart (2018) uses the term 'multi-scale ethnography' for research that tries to respond in one way or another to the desire to identify and understand cultural forms that travel across spaces, times, and levels. She describes three types of multi-scalar ethnography: multi-sited ethnography, meta-ethnography, and comparative (or vertical) case study. Multi-sited ethnography is the methodology we have chosen.

Multi-sited ethnography was originally defined by Marcus (1995, p. 105) as a methodology 'designed around chains, paths, threads, conjunctions, or juxtapositions of locations' in which ethnographers establish some form of presence based on an explicit, posited logic of association or connection among these sites. In it, as suggested by Eisenhart (2018), cultural forms produced or circulating in one locale are followed and explored in other places, with the intention of identifying and understanding connections among them and researchers, thus, quite literally follow connections, associations or relationships across specific time and space scales. Researchers might follow the interpretive logics of a group of people as they move from one site to another or the pedagogical practices of teachers as they move back and forth between their rural homes and their schooling, or the interactions of students in school and in various after-school activities (Kenway et al., 2018). However, in each case the intention is to offer a means of understanding of how activities, concerns, and needs depend on and are constrained across groups, sites, systems, and periods of time. This is also the logic we adopted to cope with and begin to collectively theorise about the variations of rurality and the relationships between education and place in rural settings.

From theory to method and back again

In addition to being collaborative, intermittent, and multi-sited, as a form of theoretically informed ethnographic studies (TIES) the project was also rooted in specific theories. These are elaborated in the individual chapters of the book, but will be briefly introduced here, to show their general roles in the design, collaboration and analytical phases of the project.

According to Willis and colleagues, theoretically informed ethnographic methodology entails being in the field among those whose lives are investigated for an extensive period of time (Willis, 2000; Willis and Trondman, 2000; Trondman, Willis and Lund, 2018). The aim is to understand and theorise the meaning of their lived experiences to bring illuminating answers to puzzling research questions that prepare the ground for social criticism and can alter both our senses of the world and capacity to see things differently. It is propelled equally by theoretical argument and empirical evidence, in a scientific analysis of cultural meaning (Willis, 2000; Trondman et al., 2018).

Our research has been informed by the theories and concepts of space developed particularly by Doreen Massey (e.g. Massey, 1994/2013). According to these theories, space is a quintessentially important concept that is understood as continuously in process and shaped through socio-spatial and material practices. Interactively, these practices both produce and contextualise the historical social relations of production, and also, by virtue of their interpellations, to some degree individual identities and actions. Actions are not purely voluntary from this theoretical position and there are close connections between space, place and the construction of social relations, practices, meaning and spatial identities.

Another key concept of our ethnographic project's theoretical framework is social class, including Marx's recognition that social classes emerge historically and contemporaneously under specific socio-historical conditions and in relation to both the development of productive forces and social division of labour. However, we have taken a somewhat broader perspective on class within the vista of Marxist class analysis than that expressed in Marx's own writing and time (e.g. Marx and Engels, 1848/1969). Like Harvey (1996), when analysing the materials related to social class we have sought a concept of class that can be used within the scope of a critical analysis of rural education and schooling in more complex social conditions than those of previous centuries. We retain interest in divisions and differences, and their consequences in terms of the development of subject identities, social rights, life conditions and future possibilities (Harvey, 1996, p. 5). However, more specifically we are also interested in how differences in education possibilities and experiences are produced and operate in class terms in different rural spaces and communities.

Like Harvey (1996) therefore, we define class in terms of human situatedness and positionality in relation to various processes of accumulation, including but not limited to economic accumulation. Capitalism arises partly through the increasing division of labour and the creation of factories, within which highly specialised production processes take place. But this division of labour does not necessarily lead to capitalism as this particular formation also requires what Marx in *Capital* called primitive accumulation: a process by which large swaths of the population were violently divorced from their traditional means of self-sufficiency through the closure of common lands. Marx described this form of accumulation as a parliamentary form of the robbery that granted landlords the rights to the people's land as private property. As Harvey (1996) notes, we all live within this historically created realm of capital and its processes of accumulation. These processes are often both very disparate and operate according to different socio-temporal scales that can only be frozen into essential identities with the force of great symbolic violence.

This idea that not all inequalities are reducible to the same categories and socio-cultural scales is highly relevant to our investigation of space and equality/inequality in education. Differences such as those of gender, ethnicity, sexuality and race are often compared to class, but they do not have the same social ontology in terms of a specific material basis in society. They exist within the class structure, but unlike (for instance) the existence of the bourgeoisie or working class, they are not specifically created by the capitalist mode of production. Capitalism could not survive without wage labour or privatisation of the means of production, but there is no exclusive relationship between any specific economic system and patriarchy (Hartmann, 1979). The gender order is certainly related to economic factors, but as previously theorised, the development of gender relations is also influenced by numerous other contextual factors, and needs to be understood in relation to local and regional variations (Connell, 1996; Connell and Messerschmidt, 2005). Hence, they cannot be reduced to assumptions of any general form, but should be actively explored in relation to the material and social conditions in a certain place. As shown by Massey (1994/2013) such variations may be substantial even between rather close localities, and she emphasises the necessity for a 'thorough going theoretical anti-essentialism at this level'.

Gender relations and associated issues have been more intensively explored in rural settings than class issues, although certainly much less than in urbanities. Studies of gender in ruralities typically present relations as more distinct, with more fixed femininities and masculinities, than in urbanities (cf. Härnsten et al., 2005) and often focus primarily on traditionally male activities and settings (Forsberg and Stenbacka, 2013). Some research also suggests that boys and young men are more likely to be included in local groupings (Waara, 2011), and rely more on social networks to provide them with future work (Öhrn, Asp-Onsjö and Holm, 2017) in rural places. For these and/or other reasons they may also tend to view their rural neighbourhood and the idea of returning after an (urban) education more favourably than girls (Svensson, 2006). Rural girls talk more about moving to urban settings and about education being the way to achieve this (Sandell, 2007; Öhrn et al., 2017). There are some indications that school content, when occasionally adjusted to local traditions, tends to align more with traditionally male than with traditionally female activities and interests (Gustafsson and Öhrn, 2012). However, some studies focused on small de-industrialised societies highlight the rather harsh effects on young men of disappearing industrial work and wage opportunities, with the consequent erosion of working-class masculinities and positive self-images (Weis, 1990; Trondman, 1995). In this respect, local conditions and kinds of rural areas may be highly relevant to analyses of social order, and associated educational issues, and differences between industrially thriving, de-industrialised and other (e.g. forested and agricultural areas) may warrant attention (cf. Forsberg and Stenbacka, 2013).

Rural inequality is one of the important and often neglected problems of social justice in our time. It is not directly reducible to capitalist accumulation or capitalist production relations, but exists within the realm of capital and the people involved live within processes that are both very disparate and operate according to different socio-temporal scales.

In accordance with the above considerations, theoretically rurality is not a passive object in our research, but it is not a fully floating signifier in the sense of being totally free from spatial relations or capitalist relations of production and accumulation. It is constituted within these relations but not determined by them. Ruralities are plural not singular and experiences and understandings of them can change teacher and student behaviour and affect educational motivation and performances, and our committed belief is that any research or theory of rurality in education must take these facets into account. Analyses rooted in such place-conscious theories of rural education relations and practices are rare (Hargreaves et al., 2009), but likely to be more valuable than studies lacking such framework to educational stakeholders, including teachers, students, their parents, local businesses and educational politicians and policymakers (Bagley and Hillyard, 2014).

As Corbett (2015) has suggested, education is as significant in and to local lives as labour or production. Moreover, like community and production relations, educational relations and experiences and understandings of them are formed in specific spatial and temporal contexts (Balfour, Mitchel and Moletsane, 2008; Bagley and Hillyard, 2014). A certain place at a certain time will always contain, mediate and foster a particular mix of social relations in particular ways in particular spaces that can be culturally observed, experienced, documented, discussed and analysed (Massey, 1994). However, the meaningfulness of the place's identity will also derive at least partially from the specificity of its interactions with spaces outside (Massey, 1994/2013; Bagley and Hillyard, 2014; Vigo and Soriano, 2014; Johansson, 2017).

This has had specific connotations for our understanding of the formation of different rural spaces and differences among them. We have identified sparsely populated areas, tourist municipalities, small industrial and small de-industrialised communities, and we have situated our research fieldwork in schools in six carefully selected places within them, where industrial capitalism has probably had different effects (Chandler, 1990; Massey, 1994/2013)). As these authors and others, for instance Harvey (1996, 2003, 2006), point out, the growth and spread of industrial capitalism led to massive reorganisation of vast areas in rural spaces in Europe such as the localities of our research. It created pockets of semi- and peri-urban industrialisation and settlement in some areas, while leaving other areas relatively untouched with their settlements remaining quite sparse. The capitalist industrialisation process has worked (and works still today) quite differently in different (types of) areas and places (and the spaces within them). It has either pushed populations out of a rural area, drawn them in or seemingly ignored them, depending on what are politically defined as predominant national economic needs and current economic climates (Balfour, Mitchell, and Moletsane, 2008). Currently the global concept of fracking is receiving great attention from multiple perspectives in these respects.

In our investigations our primary concerns have been the concomitant relations of dependency and independency on global capitalist relations of production (and corporate organisations) in particular places and the subsequent effects on education of global, national and local forces. These can be shaped by influences that seem to emanate from production directly, but also indirectly, through the construction of understandings of, and practices in, education authorities and schools, through classification and framing of curricula, and through the construction of local articulations of global pedagogical discourses. Rural spaces and their schools and school curricula are often depicted as simple, but they are in fact complex, multi-layered social constructions in respect to which understandings of local educational needs and possibilities become manifest (Balfour et al., 2008).

The role of critical theory

Massey's theories (e.g. 1994) are elements of, and influenced by, what is broadly known as critical social theory. This is concerned with the linkages, tensions, and solidarities within and between groups, in terms of dependencies and inter-dependencies across time and space and the distribution of wealth, poverty, power and influence. In our research we have attempted to connect these phenomena to educational availabilities, accessibilities, understandings, outcomes and experiences. In this sense they form the foundations for our theorisation and engagement in our research on the daily lives of people. They express convictions we have formed through iterative theoretical and empirical considerations that individuals or groups should not be represented simply as autonomous, self-contained units that can pursue their life choices unencumbered by any form of constraint (Beach, 2011). This is a similar application of critical theory and analysis in ethnography to *critical bifocality* (Weis and Fine, 2018). Critical bifocality entails simultaneous documentation of *both* the linkages and capillaries of structural arrangements *and* the local discursive and lived out practices by which privileged and marginalised youth and adults make sense of their circumstances and act within those circumstances.

Like Weis and Fine, we have engaged for some time in such research (e.g. Beach and Sernhede, 2011; Beach, Dovemark, Schwartz and Öhrn, 2013) in efforts to resolve difficulties in documenting and theorising important invisible elements of the movement and consolidation of (for example) capital, racism, and neo-liberalism in education. We regard this as crucial in order to expose and address key aspects of issues like educational justice, privilege and dispossession. In these efforts we have set out to highlight the implications of deep structural shifts in the global economy and the ways in which aspects of the new global economy can play out in educational relationships and outcomes. Similarly, in the research presented here, we have deliberately theorised about consequences of the global-level realignment of capitalism at national and local levels with regard to lived-out social and economic dynamics of individuals and collectivities, particularly in current educational relationships, experiences and lived possibilities.

From theorised analytical methodology to results

In total, the project entailed about 340 hours of classroom observations, focused on presentations of place, participation, student influence, and conflicts in the schools, as well as the presentation and positioning of places and their relations in the classification and framing of curricular content and interactions. These observations included field conversations and formal interviews with students (sixty-eight boys and sixty-eight girls) and staff at the schools, and were supplemented with observations in the local neighbourhoods and document analyses.

By undertaking ethnography we have placed emphasis on learning from informants and through this we have been particularly strong at providing details from interactions inside everyday life contexts and settings, which have been meticulously documented. This responds to points made by Walford (2018) that ethnographers are interested in the accuracy of their descriptions and analyses and try to take pains to ensure that they have sufficient evidence for all the claims they make. In line with our aims and theoretical positioning, whether and how teaching relates to place was inquired into, as was young people's views of inclusion, fellowship and conflict, and their positioning of the local school and community.

Our analyses pointed to considerable differences between the researched schools that were related to their relationships within and to the global and national political economy both broadly and in terms of local contingencies and conditions. The results are organised under a series of thematised chapter headings that try to express this. These chapters are described in the following section.

Chapter disposition

This first chapter sets the scene by presenting the research field, and some core questions for the research project relating to the dominance of urban studies in education (and social sciences more generally) and the relative silence on rural conditions and problems. The chapter also presents the research project and its theory, methodology and data production to provide a coherent background and frame for the thematic chapters so they can focus on relevant findings and discussion.

The following empirical chapters focus on prominent themes emerging from the fieldwork and address both rural schooling and youths' rural lives more generally. This is in line with the chosen theoretical understanding of place as central, and the associated requirement to analyse education, like other institutions, in its socio-spatial context.

Chapter two (*Young people about 'their' rural place: A rural idyll?*) focuses on place and draws especially on youths' presentations of the researched places. It describes the local youth understandings of the places they live and go to school in, and how these understandings may be reflected in the different strategies they envision for breaking away from and/or maintaining relationships with these places in the future. In this respect there are similarities, but also differences, between the different ruralities, especially between the sparsely populated areas and de/industrialised communities. Most notably, nature appears as a strong emerging theme among students in the sparsely populated areas, but in contrast to some previous studies, not as an uncontested idyll, and it comes with a critique against metrocentricity and its consequences for rural living.

In chapter three (*'The local place' in the pedagogic practices*) the analyses move to the different schools and their relations with the surrounding communities. Central elements of this include the presentation of the places and their relations (conflicts, values, silences) observed in teaching and their relations to other places. In this respect, the analyses indicate that teaching in the sparsely populated areas is more likely to be explicitly positioned in the rural local context, and valorise the rural positively in education exchanges, content and interaction than in the schools in small (de)industrialised communities. However, there also seem to be distinct silences on some themes and relations.

Chapter four (*Careers, agency and place. Rural students reflect on their future*) focuses on the three schools from de/industrialised communities. Whereas the previous two chapters have shown them to be similar in many ways, this chapter engage in their differences and how they reflect in the views held by young people. It shows young people's thoughts of their future options and their dreams of further education and work to relate to the local material conditions of the rural places, such as the labour markets. Classed and gendered characteristics, as well as properties of the local labour markets, were found to be particularly important in the process of shaping the young people's ideas of future careers, both limiting and broadening their views.

Chapter five (*Places and schools in times of demographic change*) reflects on migration patterns and experiences. It ties strongly with the chosen theoretical framework of the project and emphasises place as being constantly in process and sees migration as both posing challenges and providing new opportunities for sparsely populated and de-populated areas. In the researched sites there have been substantial influxes in recent years of refugees—particularly unforeseen inflows of refugees from Syria that occurred during the fieldwork. Taking this and other migrations into the areas in question as a starting point, the chapter analyses issues associated with various groups' understandings of place, education and education possibilities.

Chapter six (*Reproduction of social relations in rural schools and communities*) addresses themes of especially gender and class. It recalls previous research on gender and class in relation to rural youth and education, then presents some of the main findings from the study. These include indications of less stereotyped gender relations than in much previous research, but still an overall trend towards promotion of masculine activities and values. The findings also indicate that the centre—periphery is an important social marker that constructs social distinctions.

Chapter seven (*Education politics and rural secondary schools*) focuses on relations between rural and urban areas, as well as their respective conditions, problems and challenges. These are core issues of the book and this chapter aims to present a synthesising discussion. It draws on previous research on urban and rural youth and their schooling, and explores the under-researched rural dimension by using our data to discuss rural understandings and responses to socio-spatial issues.

The final chapter eight (*Closing discussion*) draws together central themes from the previous chapters. These are concerned with various aspects of social structures, social relations, their implications for social inclusion, and how these are addressed in schools and teaching. It also returns to the initial questions posed in the first chapters about rural-urban relations, metrocentricity and marginalisation.

References

Åberg-Bengtsson, L., (2009) The smaller the better? A review of research on small rural school in Sweden, *International Journal of Educational Research,* 48(2): 100-1098.

Andersson, A., (2003) *Inte samma lika. Identifikationer hos tonårsflickor i en multietnisk stadsdel.* [Not the same alike. Teenage girls' identifications in a multiethnic neighbourhood], Thesis, Stockholm/Stehag: Brutus Östlings Bokförlag Symposion.

Archer, L., Hollingworth, S. and Mendick, H., (2010) *Urban youth and schooling: the experiences and identities of educationally 'at risk' young people,* Maidenhead: Open Uiversity Press.

Bagley, C. and Hillyard, S., (2014) Rural schools, social capital and the Big society, *British Educational Research Journal,* 40(1): 63-78.
Balfour, R., Mitchell, C. and Moletsane, R., (2008) Troubling contexts: toward a generative theory of rurality as education research, *Journal of Rural and Community Development,* 3(3): 95-107.
Beach, D., (2011) On structure and agency in ethnographies of education: examples from this special issue and more generally, *European Journal of Educational Research,* 10(4): 572-582.
Beach, D., (2018) *Structural Injustices in Swedish Education,* Singapore: Palgrave MacMillan.
Beach, D. and Dyson, A., (2016) Tentative conclusions, in D. Beach and A. Dyson (eds.), *Equity and Education in Cold Climates.* London: Tufnell Press.
Beach, D., From, T., Johansson, M. and Öhrn, E., (2018) Education and spatial justice in rural and urban areas in three Nordic countries: A meta-ethnographic analysis, *Education Inquiry,* 9(1): 4-21.
Beach, D., Johansson, M., Öhrn, E., Rönnlund, M. and Rosvall, P.-Å., (2018) Rurality and education relations: Metro-centricity and local values in rural communities and rural schools, *European Educational Research Journal,* https://doi.org/10.1177/1474904118780420
Beach, D., Dovemark, M., Schwartz, A. and Öhrn, E., (2013) Complexities and contradictions of educational inclusion: a meta-ethnographic analysis, *Nordic Studies in Education,* 33(2): 254-268.
Beach, D. and Sernhede, O., (2011) From learning to labour to learning for marginality: school segregation and marginaliaation in Swedish suburbs, *British Journal of Sociology of Education,* 32(2): 257-274.
Chandler, A. D. Jr., (1990) *Scale and scope: The dynamics of industrial capitalism,* Cambridge: The Belknap Press.
Connell, R. W., (1996) *Gender and power,* Cambridge: Polity Press.
Connell, R. W. and Messerschmidt, J. W., (2005) Hegemonic masculinity. Rethinking the concept, *Gender and Society,* 19(6): 829-859.
Corbett, M., (2015) Towards a rural sociological imagination: ethnography and schooling in mobile modernity, *Ethnography and Education,* 10(3): 263-277.
Eisenhart, M., (2017) A matter of scale: multi-scale ethnographic research on education in the United States, *Ethnography and Education,* 12(2): 134-147.
Eisenhart, M., (2018) Changing conceptions of culture and ethnography in anthropology of education in the United States, in D. Beach, C. Bagley and S. Marques da Silva (eds.), *The handbook of ethnography of education,* London and New York: Wiley.
Eskilsson, A., (2010) *Unga utvecklar landsbygden. Uppföljning av projektet Barn på landsbygd,* Rapport från Centrum för kommunstrategiska studier (CKS), Linköpings universitet.
Farrugia, D., (2014) Towards a spatialised youth sociology: the rural and the urban in times of change, *Journal of Youth Studies,* 17(3): 293-307.
Fjellman, A.-M, Yang Hansen, K. and Beach, D., (2018) School choice and implications for equity: the new political geography of the Swedish upper secondary school market, *Educational Review,* DOI: 10.1080/00131911.2018.1457009
Forsberg, G. and Stenbacka, S., (2013) Mapping gendered ruralities, *European Countryside,* 5(1): 1-20.

Gietz-Johansen, T., (2003) Representations of ethnicity: How teachers speak about ethnic minority students, in D. Beach, T. Gordon and E. Lahelma (eds.) *Democratic Education: ethnographic challenges* (pp. 66-79), London: Tufnell.

Gudmundsson, G., (2013) Introduction: Excluded youth in itself and for itself— young people from immigrant families in Scandinavia, in G. Gudmundsson, D. Beach and V. Vestel (eds.), *Excluded youth in itself and for itself: Young people from immigrant families in Scandinavia*, London: Tufnell Press.

Gustafsson, J. and Öhrn, E., (2012) *Gender, achievement and place: Boys and masculinities in a rural area*, Paper presented at AARE, Sydney 2-6 December.

Hammersley, M. and Atkinson, P., (1983) *Ethnography: Principles in practice*, London: Tavistock.

Hargreaves, L., Kvalsund, R. and Galton, M., (2009) Reviews of research on rural schools and their communities in British and Nordic countries: Analytical perspectives and cultural meaning, *International Journal of Educational Research*, 48(2): 80-88.

Härnsten, G., Holmstrand, L., Lundmark, E., Hellsten, J.-O., Rosén, M. and Lundström, E., (2005) *Vi sätter genus på agendan: Ett deltagarorienterat projekt om flickor och pojkar i glesbygd*. [We are putting gender on the agenda: A participatory oriented project on girls and boys in sparsely populated areas]. Pedagogisk kommunikation nr 6. Växjö university: Pedagogiska institutionen.

Hartmann, H., (1979) The unhappy marriage of Marxism and feminism. Towards a more progressive union, *Capital and Class*, 3(2): 1-33.

Harvey, D. ,(1996) *Justice, nature and the geography of difference: A meta-theory for ecological socialists?* Oxford: Blackwell.

Harvey, D., (2003) *The new imperialism* (Oxford, Oxford University Press).

Harvey, D., (2006) *A brief history of neoliberalism*. New York: Oxford University Press.

Heggen, K., Myklebust, J. O and Øia, T., (2001) (eds). *Ungdom: I spenninga mellom det lokale og det globale*. [Youth: In tension between the local and the global], Oslo: Det norske samlaget.

Holm, A.-S., (2008) *Relationer i skolan. En studie av femininiteter och maskuliniteter i år 9*. [Relations in school. A study of femininities and masculinities in the 9th grade], Thesis, Göteborg: Acta Universitatis Gothoburgensis.

Jeffrey, B. and Troman, G., (2004) Time for ethnography, *British Journal of Educational Research*, 30(4): 535-548.

Johansson, M., (2017) "Yes, the power is in the town": An ethnographic study of student participation in a rural Swedish secondary school, *Australian and International Journal of Rural Education*, 27(2): 61-76.

Kennelly, J. and Dillabough, J.-A., (2008) Young people mobilizing the language of citizenship: struggles for classification and new meaning in an uncertain world, *British Journal of Sociology of Education*, 29(5): 493-508.

Kenway, J., Fahey, J., Epstein, D., Koh, A., McCarthy, C. and Rizvi, F., (2018) Multi-sited global ethnography and elite schools: a methodological entrée, in D. Beach, C. Bagley and S. Marques da Silva (eds.), *The Handbook of Ethnography of Education*, London and New York: Wiley.

Lindbäck, J. and Sernhede, O., (2010) Det 'integrerade' gymnasiet och den segregerade staden. Elevers berättler om det urbana rummet och platsens betydelse. [The segregated city and the school as a multicultural meeting grouund. Upper secondary pupils and their narratives on urban space and the significance of place], *Utbildning och Demokrati*, 19(1): 73-92.

Marcus, G. E., (1995). Ethnography in/of the world system: the emergence of multi-sited ethnography, *Annual Review of Anthropology,* 24(1): 95-117.
Marklund, I., (2000) *Skolan mitt i byn,* Östersund: Glesbygdsverket.
Marx, K and Engels, F., (1848/1969) *Selected works, vol. one* [pp. 98-137). Moscow: Progress Publishers.
Massey, D., (1994/2013) *Space, place and gender*, Cambridge: Polity Press.
Möller, P., (2011) (ed.). *Vem bygger landet?* [Who builds the country?]. Vilnius: Gidlunds förlag.
Nolan, K. and Anyon, J., (2004) Learning to do time: Willis's model of cultural reproduction in an era of postindustralism, globalization and mass incarceration, in N. Dolby, G. Dimitriadis and P. Willis (eds.), *Learning to labor in new times*, New York: RoutledgeFalmer.
Öhrn, E., (2011) Class and ethnicity at work. Segregation and conflict in a Swedish secondary school, *Education Inquiry, 2*(2): 345-357.
Öhrn, E., (2012a) Making a difference. Targets and resources for student influence, in T. Strand and M. Roos (eds.), *Education for social justice, equity and diversity* (pp. 19-36), Münster: LIT Verlag.
Öhrn, E., (2012b) Urban education and segregation: the responses from young people, *European Educational Research Journal,* 1(1): 45-57.
Öhrn, E., Asp-Onsjö, L. and Holm, A-S., (2017) Discourses on gender and achievement in lower secondary education, in K. Kantasalmi and G. Holm (eds.), *The State, Schooling and Identity: Diversifying Education in Europe* (pp. 173-192), London: Palgrave Macmillan.
Öhrn, E. and Weiner, G., (2007) Urban education in Europe: section editors' introduction, in W. T. Pink and G. W. Noblit (eds.), *International handbook of urban education* (pp. 397-411), Dordrecht: Springer.
Sandell, A., (2007) *Utbildningssegregation och självsortering. Om gymnasieval, genus och lokala praktiker,* [Segregation and self-sorting in eduction: on choice of upper secondary education, gender and local practices], Thesis, Malmö University College.
Schwartz, A. and Öhrn, E., (2012) Fellowship and solidarity? in W. T.. Pink (ed.), *Schools and Marginalized youth: an international perspective,* Cresshill, NJ: Hampton Press.
Sernhede, O., (2007). Territorial stigmatisation. Hip hop and informal schooling, in W. T. Pink and G. W. Noblit (eds.), *International handbook of urban education* (pp. 463-479), Dordrecht: Springer.
SKL, (2011) *Kommungruppsindelning 2011*, Stockholm: Sveriges Kommuner och Landsting.
Solstad, K. J., (2009) The impact of globalisation on small communities and small schools in Europe, in T. Lyons, J.-Y. Choi and G. McPhan (eds.), *Proceedings from international symposium for innovation in rural education*, University of New England, Australien.
Swedish National Board for Youth Affairs, (2010) *Fokus 10. En analys av ungas inflytande*, [Focus 10. An analysis of youth influence], Ungdomsstyrelsens skrifter 2010:10, Stockholm: Ungdomsstyrelsen.
Svensson, L., (2006) *Vinna och försvinna? Drivkrafter bakom ungdomars utflyttning från mindre orter* [Where do the winners go?: Driving forces behind youth leaving smaller localities], Thesis, Linköping Studies in Arts and Science No 359, Linköpings universitet.
Svensson, L., (2010) Var du bor spelar roll—landsort eller storstad. [Where you live matters—the countryside or the city], in Ungdomsstyrelsen (eds.), *Fokus 10. En analys av ungas inflytande,* Stockholm: Ungdomsstyrelsen.

Troman, G., (2006) Editorial, *Ethnography and Education* 1(1): 1-2.
Trondman, M., (1995) Vem talar för framtidens förlorare? [Who speaks for the future losers?], in G. Bolin and K. Lövgren (eds.), *Om unga män*. Lund: Studentlitteratur.
Trondman, M., Willis, P. and Lund, A.,, (2018) Lived forms of schooling: bringing the elementary forms of ethnography to the science of education, in D. Beach, C. Bagley and S. Marques da Silva (eds.), *The Handbook of Ethnography of Education*, London and New York: Wiley.
Vigo Arrazola, B and Soriano Bozalongo, J. (2014) Teaching practices and teachers' perceptions of group creative practices in inclusive rural schools, *Ethnography and Education*, 9(2): 253-269.
Waara, P., (2011) Mellan något och någon—forskning om ungdom på landsbygden. [Between something and someone—research on youth in the countryside], in P. Möller (ed.), *Vem bygger landet?* Vilnius: Gidlunds förlag.
Wacquant, L., (2007) Territorial stigmatization in the age of advanced marginality, *Thesis 11*, 91(1): 66-77.
Walford, G., (2018) Recognisable continuity. A defence of multiple methods, in D. Beach, C. Bagley and S. Marques da Silva (eds.), *The handbook of ethnography of education*, Londen and New York: Wiley.
Weis, L., (1990) *Working class without work. High school students in a de-industrializing economy*, New York: Routledge.
Weis, L. and Fine, M., (2018) Critical bifocality, in D. Beach, C. Bagley and S. Marques da Silva (eds.), *The Handook of Ethnography of Education*, London and New York: Wiley.
Willis, P., (2000) *The ethnographic imagination*, Cambridge: Polity Press
Willis, P. and Trondman, M., (2000) Manifesto for ethnography, *Ethnography*, 1(1): 5-16.

Chapter 2

Young people talk about *their* rural place: A rural idyll?

Per-Åke Rosvall and Maria Rönnlund

Introduction

In this chapter we analyse how young people talked about the place they lived and the spaces in which they interacted. In line with Massey (1994), we think that social interactions take place somewhere in a physical sense and thus they necessarily have a spatial form. Some of these interactions and relations 'will be contained within the place, others will stretch beyond it, tying any particular locality into wider relations and processes in which other places are implicated too' (see Massey, 1994, p. 120). In addition, this chapter draws extensively upon Massey's concept of power geometry, in which localities are understood as imagined, produced and maintained against social, material and environmental grounds (see also Moskal, 2015). The youths' social, mental and physical spaces and their agency within those spaces depends on the number and quality of their interactions—what might be termed the *localised rituals* used to organise their power over places. This chapter deals with questions of how young people see *their* rural areas. What was valued and what was not valued? How did they understand their local place and its relations to other places? The interviews with the students in the rural schools were done in an ethnographic tradition; we were trying to learn from the participants rather than coming with a formalised set of questions. The students were asked questions such as 'What is it like to live here?' and 'What do you do in school?' Through those intentionally loose opening questions and the informal conversations that followed we tried to find out what they did, with whom and where, and how they valued those activities. This ethnographic research based on interviews and fieldwork adds value to the literature since most previous rural researchers have used surveys (Valentine, 1997; Matthews et al., 2000; Krivokapic-Skoko and Collins, 2016) or more structured interviews which might rule out questions of importance to the participant but not thought of by the researcher. There is some rural research with a focus on education with a more open approach, although this work seldom puts education in a wider context (Åberg-Bengtsson, 2009; Corbett, 2013) we address that shortcoming here.

Earlier research and the theoretical background

Within the literature there are some vigorous debates on the analytical tools or concepts which can be used in order to understand place in late modernity. Some describe a contemporary cosmopolitan youth culture (Waldron, 1992; Vertovec and Cohen, 2002; Youdell, 2004) where youth is seen as independent of the local and unlimited within the global. However, the concept of cosmopolitanism has several other associations. When we use the concept in this text we refer to a practice that is independent of place and social relations, and to a competence in adapting to new places and cultures. In relation to cosmopolitanism, electronic mediation is often understood as an important vehicle in nurturing social relations independent of place, and understanding and adapting to new places and cultures (Appadurai, 1995). There are, however, emerging critiques of these understandings of a cosmopolitan youth culture which is independent of place and seeks opportunities nation- and worldwide. These critiques argue that the concept of cosmopolitan youth merely refers to an upper middle class positioned in the centre, while working-class youth geographically positioned outside of cities have other opportunities (Youdell, 2004).

Much research into rural contexts points at the strong social, physical and mental attachments of individuals to the place where they live; the concept of the 'rural idyll' has been used to explain the strength of these attachments. The rural idyll encompasses a certain mentality of relaxed generosity; social relations where everyone knows everyone else, whatever their age or generation; and minimal physical and socioeconomic segregation—cities and city life are often described with exactly the opposite attributes (Halfacree, 1995; Rye, 2006; Leyshon, 2008; Stenbacka, 2016). There is, nevertheless, some research that describes rural life as harsh, with few options other than to migrate to places with more employment opportunities and up-scaled infrastructure (Corbett, 2013; Paulgaard, 2017; Sørensen and Pless, 2017). In our interviews we can, as in previous research, read descriptions that closely correspond to the notion of the rural idyll; however, our ethnographic method also allowed us to see what we in this chapter call *cracks in the idyll*, i.e. what might be a more realistic portrayal of rural places, not as idylls but rather as places where economic life in particular was described as harder than in other areas.

Youth is both affected by how interactions are socially and materially valued as well as being themselves producers of value when engaged in localised practices. Our first section in this chapter presents what seemed to be valued by the youth.

However, as the analytical concepts of space and place implies, what was valued shifted and varied between individuals and contexts. A valued materialised place is naturally intertwined with social spaces, and also provides opportunities for the mental space to conceive of what is actually possible (Gordon et al., 2000). In seeking to explain how students talked about their understanding of their physical, social and mental spaces, our analysis considers all activities taking place in the local community, but it should be stressed that school and education is particularly important to understanding young people's articulated sense of place; after all, schools were our main research sites and the places where the young people spent most of their time during weekdays.

The first impression—a rural idyll?

We will now present our results and will do so in relation to explaining how the analysis emerged. Our first conclusions fitted quite well into earlier descriptions of the rural idyll; however, upon deeper analysis *cracks in the idyll* emerged, significant fissures which will be presented in the second results section.

The first—often poignant—theme that emerged from the material was the positive voices of rural youth: 'I kind of like the place and the individuals who live here.' 'Even though I know that I have to leave to get the job that I want, I think of this place as a place that I will return to.' 'It is not as stressful here as in the town.' 'My family has a history that is important to me here.' These excerpts from some of the interviews give a relatively positive portrayal of the rural places under study. There were, of course, contradictory views (indeed sometimes expressed by the same individual), but overall the positive expressions still stand out. The first series of extracts from conversations with young people which we present here do convey a commonly shared sense of 'their place' as a rural idyll. However, since each site provided different possibilities for social inclusion and agency the young people constructed their identities in relation to clearly distinct realities—there is no united 'voice of the young rural community'.

Social relationships: Everyone knows everyone

There was a common understanding among most of the young people that everyone knew everyone, which in most cases was seen as something positive:

> I say hello to everything and everyone, it doesn't matter if I've seen them before or know them, it doesn't matter. And if you compare that with the city [...] in the city you don't say hello to people you meet [...] So, it's a

difference, you get a bit more enclosed and isolated there, like for example when you ride the city bus. So even though there are many more people in the city, you become more enclosed and by yourself.

(Coastal School, February 25)

The notion of everyone knowing everyone was also held to be a certain mentality, manifested for example, through good behaviour:

Since I live where I live [some distance away from the school village], after school I'm with my family and those living nearby. Then you learn to respect others. I mean you can't do someone great harm without apologising since you see them all the time.

(Mountain School, November 9)

Good behaviour was, as in the research of Halfacree (1995) and Svendsen and Svendsen (2016), closely related to the context of people living in a rural place. This excerpt could, of course, be interpreted as both positive and negative: positive because the interviewee thinks twice and behaves well on the one hand, and negative in the sense of it being a critique of a regulating practice on the other. However, listening to the recording you can hear the warm tone of the voice; clearly, the speaker thinks of it as something positive. This also seemed important in how the interviewees portrayed themselves in relation to others—as more relaxed and welcoming than those from larger cities which most portrayed as stressed and anonymous: 'they [people in the cities] do not even say hello to their neighbour' (cf. Smith and Higley, 2012). Krister from Coastal School also argued that friends in rural areas become closer than their urban counterparts:

In the city you may get more friends, but here I think you get closer friends, closer but fewer.

(Coastal School, February 18)

Socialising between age groups and generations was common. Two boys in different, sparsely populated areas mentioned that they played bridge with older people. Quite a few mentioned that knowing everyone did not only mean knowing everyone in your age but also knowing older people:

> You know it can take almost two hours to go to the supermarket to buy a litre of milk. You talk to almost everyone you meet. The old ones too.
> (Mountain School, February 26)

This was not only mentioned in interviews; it was also observed during fieldwork:

> I have met grandmas and grandads of the students at school and grandchildren of teachers. Today I also met a student and his grandad on their way from the forest where they had been working.
> (Forest School, May 5)

In the areas outside the school villages it was common for interviewees to refer to practical reasons to explain why they played with others in classes over or below their own. An excerpt from the interview with Magnus relates to this:

> They are the only ones about my age in my village. It has always been us playing since preschool, ehh, or Madelene of course started secondary school one year before me and Milo one year after, but we still meet after school when we come home.
> (Mountain School, November 3)

In other words, there was a common understanding of everyone knows everyone. Although this holds for both those who commuted to school and those who did not, it was more common that those commuting said that they viewed their closest family as the main source for their social relations (cf. Rönnlund, 2019).

Local place, nature and uniqueness

The surrounding natural world played an important role for many of the interviewed students, both in activities with peers and for doing things individually or with the family. The connection to nature and activities practised outdoors were more emphasised in the three sparsely populated areas (Mountain, Inland and Forest) even though there were examples of the same in River, Sea and Coastal. Interviewees from the Mountain, Inland and Forest communities frequently mentioned hunting, snow mobile driving and hiking for example.

Interviewer:	What is it that is good about living here?
Fredrika:	Yes you get a lot of fresh air and you can have the finest and cleanest water and you can get away from all technology if you go to a summer cabin and I do that quite often. (…).
Felicia:	It is nice nature too!
Interviewer:	Yes it was this with nature. What are you doing when you not are in school?
Fredrika:	Well now a friend and I are building a cabin (*koja*) with a lot of planks that we found where there had been a sawmill. So we took those planks and we have made the floor and we have installed a toilet and there is a stream where we can bathe.

(Forest School, May 3)

Outdoor activities were sometimes related to a family-owned country home or mountain cabin; references to the latter were most common in the material collected from Mountain:

> During the winter I don't have that much time to spend with my peers at the weekends. My family usually go to our mountain cabin.
> (Mountain School, October 27)

Even though references to a family cabin were more scarce in the de/industrialised communities, Chris, a girl living in one of those municipalities (Coastal), did make the following comments:

> Where I live there are only a few houses, grandma and grandad, and siblings of my parents live there. All of us also have a cabin each one kilometre away in the woods. We used to celebrate midsummer and Easter there. Then we can be with each other.
> (Coastal School, February 27)

Even though Chris lived in a de/industrialised community her family owned a cabin, and thus she has something in common with those living in the three sparsely populated areas. This example shows the importance of seeing variation not only *between* the research sites and how they are defined as sparsely and de/industrialised areas: it is also important to point to the fact that the empirical findings varied *within* the individual research sites.

Despite the example of Chris, closeness to nature was more apparent among the students resident in the three sparsely populated areas when constructing their sense of rural place. In those areas nature was also used when constructing the misconceptions of those outside, for example in relation to hunting. In Forest School the issue of whether or not to hunt wolves raised a question that was keenly discussed and offered the possibility of something to unite around and construct an outsider:

> Well, this with the wolves, I don't think they [the people in urban areas] really understand how hard this is for us. We don't have so much food and shops here. We have nothing of this and we mostly hunt our food. And everything is almost gone; the wolves take it all. (Forest School, April 20)

> Yes, the power is in the town. And they decide a lot without knowing how it is in reality. (Forest School, May 6)

The construction of an outsider and articulating an urban critique could thus create a sense of belonging. In this sense, nature is used as a source for creating and defining themselves as different to the centre, or to individuals in the town. In one of the excerpts above one of the students also claims to know more about *reality*. Knowing more about reality also implies a critique of the urban as not really being real (see further chapter seven).

Another recurrent theme in the interviews was the local place and what happened there to make it distinct and unique. In five of the six research sites the young people referred to a summer and/or winter fair as important events. In the River community the big summer fair lasted a whole week, with market stalls, roller coasters and different competitions; the fair finished with a live music event on the final Saturday, with dance music for the older folks and a concert including a famous Swedish artist for the young adults. Jessica put the Inland fair in the context of a place being something and having its own intrinsic meaning:

> People think that Inland is really small and that it is nothing. But if you live here and see all the activities that are around, and that there are market fairs, then I think they would think of Inland as big enough. The first impression used to be that Inland is nothing, but it is more than it looks like at first sight. (Inland School, October 22)

The young people referred to the fair as 'putting their place on the map' since people from the surrounding villages and even towns came to visit. Some also referred to individuals born in the village but now living elsewhere taking the chance to visit their former 'home village' and relatives and friends there. There were also other events that the students referred to as important, such as sport events:

> The older students at Forest School were active as volunteers, with a small *salary* given to the class for a big international world championship held close to the village where the school is situated. In that way, the students in these classes could earn some money together. Many of the students talked a lot about their participation in this event and they seemed to be proud to be part of this activity, which was also economically important for the area.   (Forest School, May 5)

Nature, the locality itself and things that happened there were important themes when representing the local place; however, more emphasis was put on these factors in the three sparsely populated areas. Important social events (that could be construed as neutral) together with other unique elements of rural life were fused together in a dual construct and set against a cultural elite living elsewhere and not understanding the harshness of nature and rural life. In short, we may discern a defensive critique of the city and the urban way of living. Nevertheless, it can be argued that nature is also used to construct a more positive understanding of the self as essentially rural, and local events as defining a rural place or community.

The basis used to develop notions of the rural idyll

Almost all of the young people then, talked positively about the place they lived in and the social relationships they had there. This was, however, more heavily emphasised in the three sparsely populated areas and more specifically articulated in terms of activities related to the locale, for example being out on the mountain, fishing, hunting or going to the local summer or winter fair. People valued the geographical place, the things they could do there and the prevailing social relations. Again, many of the concepts used by the young people could be associated with traditional notions of a rural idyll. In light of this, it is interesting to analyse what platforms or on what basis they developed these notions; doing so will reveal something about what was held dear by the young people and their chances of nurturing these values in their future lives.

The school where the young people spent most of their time together was, of course, very important in this respect. Here, they expressed common understandings of the local place. Some things could be talked about in both positive and negative ways, such as 'it is too quiet, there is nothing to do', but on the other hand, 'it is calm here, there is not so much stress.'

> It is the first day after the autumn break. The students talk about what they have been doing during the holiday. I am quite surprised that so many of them say that they have been resting. One boy says that he has not done much more than laying on the kitchen couch. It is articulated in such a way that it seems a valued thing to do.
> (Mountain School, November 13)

The young people themselves were important mediators of the rural values, but so were the teachers and the interior of the schools. There were differences between the three small de/industrialised communities and the three sparsely populated areas in terms of how the local place was referred to and how the interior of the schools acknowledged and reflected local circumstances (see next chapter).

Another common feature that was mentioned as being important for feeling socially connected to the local place was sports; for example Kristina:

> In the football team [...] we've found something that we all like, it's something we have in common and that's what I like about it.
> (Coastal School, February 25)

In fact, most of the young people—boys especially, but also girls—practised some sort of sport. There were some general differences between the communities so far as which sports were played, and there were also some differences of frequency and activity between girls and boys. Boys engaged in team sports to a greater extent and seemed to practise their sport more frequently. There were also both boys and girls seriously aiming for the national team in their sport, all the way down to those practising sport or a training activity just once in a while or not at all. For all youth, local traditions played a crucial role when it came to sports, especially team sports. For example, in Mountain community there had been both a boys' team in indoor hockey (*innebandy*) and ice hockey, a fact which was commented on by the boys in the class:

> Previously we had an ice hockey team but due to political decisions they restored the ice arena in Low valley just before they had to turn down the industry there. There are almost no youth living in Low valley anymore so the teams declined because there were not enough people that could or wanted to commute there. Now it is only floor-ball [a kind of indoor hockey] and even then there are not enough players to form teams in each age group. (Mountain School, December 14)

Even though there was not exactly a plethora of opportunities to practise sports, most of the youth engaging with sport seemed satisfied with the choice they had made. An exception might be the girls in Forest School who claimed that to exercise their interest in dancing they had to travel too far, which obviously was a limitation, not an opportunity. Even though there were a few aiming high with ambitions of representing Sweden, most students mentioned the social dimensions of sport to be of most importance.

Apart from sports, fishing, hunting and snow mobile driving were often mentioned as important leisure time activities, especially in the three sparsely popluated areas; analysis of those particular activities are developed in chapter five. There were some additional activities arranged for young people by the local authorities, organisations and associations (youth club activities, church youth departments, etc.), particularly in the de/industrialised municipalities. However, the overall impression was that organised sports dominated, and there were in general few other *arranged* things going on as leisure time activities. Quite a few of the students said that there was nothing to do, but when asked what they actually did, their leisure time was in most cases filled with activities. Some activities were referred to by the students as doing nothing, even though they actually did something and made an effort to go somewhere to do so. To meet at John's store for the young people in Mountain village, was one such example:

> We usually meet at John's store, they have a few tables and chairs where people can fill in their betting slips. Some of us buy some candy, however, they usually let us sit there even though we do not buy anything. It is nice of them, because they really do not have to.
> (Mountain School, November 12)

This excerpt is interesting in two ways: it illustrates how a local place is used as a venue to meet and also how generosity, which according to Halfacree (1995) is usually associated with a rural mentality, is used to describe the staff working at John's store. Having nothing to do and 'taking it easy' could also be viewed as something positive (cf. Rönnlund, 2019). Furthermore, when something did happen and people were creative in organising social events, it was usually quite easy to gather peers (especially in summer time) since there were not many other things to compete with:

> Everyone in the class is connected to the same chat group and in the summer it usually only take a short while to gather people if we start a fire for a barbeque at the lake. (Mountain School, December 14)

In this excerpt social media (the chat group) is mentioned as the platform that keeps peers together. Social media is usually understood as useful for building cosmopolitan bonds. However, our findings contest, for example, Appadurai's (1995) conclusions, which describe the ways in which emplaced communities become extended via the geographical mobility of their inhabitants and electronic mediation. Appadurai (1995 p. 213) argues that electronic mediation is a powerful force in overcoming what many people face as increasing difficulties of relating to, or indeed producing, *locality* ('as a structure of feeling, a property of life and an ideology of situated community'). Relating his argument to our research is difficult as we found few clear examples of observations or statements that support his conclusions. This could be due to contextual differences, although looking at the empirical data from a distance it is possible to argue that Appadurai's argument is both confirmed and contested. For instance, few of the students when asked said that they used social media (Appadurai uses the concept of electronic mediation, which includes social media) for interaction with people in other places. Some said that they used social media to keep up with relatives or friends that had moved away or friends and relatives that they had left behind. However, most referred to interaction with class peers via social media or gaming, as Maria (first excerpt) and Roger below:

> Malin lives far away and I live in the village next to Mountain village. In the evenings we use social media to talk and chat with each other.
> (Mountain School, November 11)

Interviewer: What do you do after school?
Roger: Gaming. If we can't meet we connect to an interactive game as a team and game together. (River School, May 4).

When following bloggers some referred to the importance of knowing the person beforehand:

Rina: I read some gym blogs to get inspiration for training.
Interviewer: Who writes the blog?
Rina: I guess you don't know her. She used to work at the gym where I train, but she moved. But I know she does good stuff.
(River School, April 7)

Only a few students referred to using social media to interact on a regular basis with individuals whom they had not met in person beforehand. In other words, social media was used to maintain and develop existing social relationships, or to keep up to date with local prominent individuals; it was not used to the same extent to nurture national or cosmopolitan bonds. Social media can thus first and foremost be understood as a basis for developing a local community, to keep in touch with local citizens. However, this is not to forget that some students also referred to gaming or chatting with national and international friends whom they had never met.

In conclusion, three major vehicles function as platforms or serve as the basis for developing a valued notion of the local place: the school, leisure time activities (mainly sports) and social media. They all provide, to different degrees and with different emphases, the basis for mental, social and physical attachments. Platforms such as social media mostly seemed to work as a mediator to keep in contact with peers or informed about developments in the localities, while interactions in school could work more visibly as a mediator of the rural idyll.

Cracks in the idyll?

As stated above, our first impression during the analysis in large part corresponded with the findings of Halfacree (1995) and other rural researchers (Rye, 2006): there was a 'relatively coherent social grouping with respect to rural social representations' [as a rural idyll] (Halfacreee, 1995, p. 19). However, reading our field notes and listening to interviews over and over again, it became clear that what had initially been faintly heard, but not fully acknowledged in the strong Arcadian buzz, was that the young people did not solely describe a rural idyll, as previous research has sometimes asserted (Halfacree, 1995; Rye, 2006). In fact, listening back to their conversations showed that they often presented the notion of the idyll in relation to a critique of, for example, everyone knows everyone or of living close to nature. Evidently, descriptions of their areas as rural idylls were not clear-cut and uncontested.

In most cases, the young people naturally made comparisons—sometimes sharply critical—between their home villages and other places. Most of the youths commuting to school firstly mentioned how their home village differed from the town where the school was situated. Secondly, they referred to places further away which was the most common first point of comparison for those living in the school village. Commonly, the home village was described as 'smaller than X town', or criticised as there was 'less to do here than in Y town'. Whatever the starting point, the descriptions lead to the conclusion that power is seen to be at the centre; or, as stated elsewhere, 'the power is in the town' (Johansson, 2017), implying a discourse of hegemonic metrocentrism. Interestingly, the centre or the town did not mean a particular place but rather came in sequences as the nearest bigger place or town and then the next town larger than that and so on, as in a larger place inland then a larger town by the coast, for example Stockholm or Berlin (or another town if they extended their comparison abroad). A common expression of those living in the inland communities was *the coast*, a place where power resided in terms of economics and where things *happened*, where one could get educated and, contrary to the deeply rural areas, where there were a variety of job opportunities.

Social relationships: Did everyone really know everyone and how well?

Most of the students seemed unaware of social background as a structuring force. The discourse of 'everyone knows everyone' was pervasive and seemed to make the young people more or less surprised at the thought that someone might have more material, social or cultural resources at their disposal. We only have a few such examples when students notes that some might have a stronger material base, as in the following where Magnus noting where might be more attractive to live:

> *Interviewer:* Would you say that it is more attractive to live somewhere in Mountain?

Magnus: No, I'm not sure but maybe it is a little bit more attractive to live at X street close to the lake. Most of them have their own businesses. They buy a new snow mobile every year [laughter].
(Mountain School, November 10)

The discourse of everyone knows everyone was strong among the youth in all rural communities but markedly so in the three sparsely populated areas. When asked further about what impact it really had they referred to both good and bad things ('you feel safe', 'you cannot do anything without everyone knowing' and so forth), but most referred to it as a good thing. However, when asked for explicit examples many changed their minds:

> You do not know them really. You know who they are and who their relatives are. You ask them how it is with their cousin or such like but you don't know much more than he plays football and scored in the last game. You don't *really* know them. (River School, April 8)

When asked if they had ever used the opportunity that everyone knows everyone to get something changed in their local community they answered that they had not:

> When my classmate's father became chairman of the municipality I thought that we would try to influence my classmate to ask favours from his father, to get a place for us to meet after school finishes for example. It kind of never happened. I don't know why.
> (Mountain School, November 10)

On the other hand, another boy said that when they talk to someone they know they might not think of it as trying to influence things in a certain direction:

> We were at Ronny's home yesterday. Ronny's father is responsible for the ice arena (*ishallen*). We talked with him about how the ice arena could be improved. But I really didn't think of that as influence.
> (Mountain School, December 12)

Everyone knowing everyone seemed to affect how they imagined themselves as open-minded and inclusive; however, there were also some scepticism of whether individuals 'really knew' each other and—as in the previous quote—if knowing everyone actually mattered when it came to influencing important things.

Everyone knowing everyone in most cases came with positive associations, but problems—such as never being anonymous—were also mentioned. Quite a few said that if they had done something embarrassing 'everyone knew' the day after and the episode often felt exaggerated. Some said that this was one of the bad things that came along with the good things of living in a rural area. However, there were a few that thought of the notion of everyone knowing everyone as inherently problematic:

> If I tell something to a friend or friends then half of Inland knows it within the next week. Everyone gossips here. I hate it! It feels that you can't say anything to anyone. [...] That can be dreadful. There are people that know more about me than me myself. It has also happened a number of times that people have said things about me that simply are not true, just to make them look better themselves. (Inland School, November 18)

Even though most young people referred to everyone knows everyone as a positive aspect of the rural mentality, their openness was tested when it came to interacting with immigrants. In River, Mountain, Sea and Coastal Schools there were quite a few immigrants, most of them having arrived in 2015. The organisation of newly arrived immigrants differed significantly. In River, Sea and Coastal School the immigrants were integrated in ordinary classes as soon as possible (most commonly Crafts, Physics, Mathematics, Art), while in Mountain school immigrant students had their own classes in a separate classroom. In the Inland and Forest Schools there were also some labour immigrants (so-called *green wave* immigrants). From observations made in all schools it could be seen that there were only a few interactions between *inborn* students and immigrants from outside Europe, while European green wave immigrants seemed to be more integrated. In River School, for example (cf. Rosvall, 2017), this situation was clearly visible since one of the public spaces was two stories tall and had a corridor on the second floor which most students used in order to get to the dining hall during lunch; they could look down on the students in the public space, with a different sports table. This space was almost always occupied by immigrants. When the *inborn* students were asked about this in relation to the notion of everyone knows everyone there were different kinds of responses: 'Yes I know, but I do sports with them', or 'I have not thought of that', or 'oh, I did not think of them, I thought of those who lived here for a long time.' Immigrants did not, in other words, seem fully involved in the concept of 'everyone knows everyone'. As in one of the examples cited here, sports were commonly put forward, both by the young people and teachers, as having a positive impact on integration. However, it came as a surprise to the interviewer when an immigrant was mentioned as being integrated through sports, since interactions between inborn students and the immigrant mentioned had, apart from a few occasions, rarely been observed in classroom situations. In other words, integration through sports did not in the end mean integration everywhere else. This might not come as a surprise since research has shown that integration processes seem difficult almost everywhere (Bevelander and Pendakur, 2014; Bunar and Ambrose, 2016), not just in rural areas. Still, it was interesting to see who were included in the notion of everyone knows everyone. Two immigrant boys in River said in the interview that they did not think it was much to do with the segregation between immigrants and inborn; however, they hoped that they could stay in River since they thought of it as a place with fewer and less intense conflicts than in the south (i.e. Stockholm) (cf. Rosvall, 2017).

Nature and place

In light of our further analysis the initially prominent discourse of the rural idyll rather seemed as a counter discourse set against discourses the students thought of as produced in more central/city areas. The rural idyll seemed to be used in order to equalise power relations. When thinking of the future the students' descriptions were in sharp contrast to those of an idyll, and few saw opportunities to get a job or fulfil their dreams in the rural place where they lived (Rönnlund et al., 2017). In fact, few saw any chance of living in the area when they were adults (Rönnlund, 2018). A few made strategic educational and vocational choices in order to stay in their local place (see chapter four). The majority of those who expressed a wish to stay were in the main those who knew that they would inherit property or a firm and thus felt secure, for example by knowing that in due course they would take over the family farm. Material resources such as land ownership were important in shaping how the young people could imagine themselves related to the place in the future. Even though Sweden has *the right of common access* that gives everyone right to access nature, landowner or not, variations in economic and social resources still made a difference. Basically, it was easier for those who owned a mountain cabin or summer house or knew someone who did. In addition, in the northern communities access to a snow mobile was vital during winter:

Interviewer: You seem to use your snow mobiles quite often.
Fredrika: Yes, and a snow mobile costs a lot, about one hundred thousand [9,000 EUR].
Interviewer: For a snow mobile that you use for leisure? Oh my!
Felicia: Yes, and we bought one and it was like, hundred, hundred twenty or hundred thirty thousand [9,000-12000 EUR]
Interviewer: You could have bought a reasonable car.
Fredrika: But everyone goes for it, cars, snowmobile and hunting.
Felicia: Everyone has a snow mobile or hunts. It is a given when you live here. It is as a car in other places. If you don't have a snow mobile you lend one from your neighbour.

(Forest School, May 3)

The excerpt touches on the status of cars, snow mobiles and hunting, as well as the considerable financial requirements needed in order to obtain a new snow mobile; it is simple—if you do not have the wherewithal you do not have a snow mobile, and you will need a kind neighbour who is not using his or hers to help you out.

Simply being in the mountain hut was an activity that often came across in the interviews with those in the northern, sparsely populated areas. Among those students with access to a mountain cabin or summer house, it was common to refer to these places as a physical attachment and to see them as a possible future route back to their local community. Even though no one mentioned the lack of such resources as a problem, it is obvious that physical attachments in this form might make for an advantage in terms of establishing physical, social and mental bonds, i.e. those with this material resource are clearly privileged.

Living close to nature in sparsely populated areas also came with difficulties in terms of commuting. In all research sites there were examples of students talking about the problems of commuting to school, to visit peers or practise sports (cf. Cedering, 2016). This was especially so in Forest, where almost none of the students lived in the school village:

It is quite a long distance to everything so, for example, we play soccer but we can't train very many times every week. Because it is such long distances and if we had to travel so much every week it is not possible. It is 150 kilometres between the two players who live in the north and south. (Forest School, 23 May)

Most of the young people in our study seemed to think of their rural place in a positive but realistic manner, seeing—and celebrating—its idyllic aspects but also acknowledging its difficulties as well—the tiresome commuting and adverse economics, a pleasant temporal space in which they lived but few imagined their future in. There were a few, often with significant economic resources to draw on, that imagined themselves with a future in the local place but those can be seen as exceptions (see chapter four). It would be useful to remind ourselves at this point of Massey's power geometry: 'some people are more in charge of it than others; some initiate flows and movement, others don't' (1994, p. 149). According to Massey's statement the rural young people in our six research communities could by no means be said to initiate such flows; with a few exceptions, late 20th century Swedish neoliberal economics and politics have led to challenging, arguably highly damaging, consequences—school closures, the flight of job opportunities and the baleful influences of individualism and rootless and restless cosmopolitanism (especially the notion of high mobility). Even though the young people in our study seemed to be mentally, socially and physically attached to their place they also seemed to be literally marinated in *central* discourses of being individually, socially and geographically independent: the cosmopolitan mentality of moving if necessary to get an education, a job or to fulfil career dreams has even taken root among the rural young people in our study.

What is the basis for notions of the rural idyll?

As explained earlier, we think that schools, local places and social media are important platforms to produce (and reproduce) notions of a valued place in which to live and work. If we start with the schools it is important to highlight the differences between the sparsely populated areas and the small deindustrialised communities. Producing notions of a rural idyll was not the only thing going on in the schools. They were also producing notions which could be understood as devaluing the rural, especially what Corbett (2005) refers to as the notion of 'learning to leave'. For most of the young people the transition from compulsory school to upper secondary would include a transition in place, since few of the rural communities had an upper secondary school. However, this was taken as self-evident and the continuation of developing valued resources such as social networks or being close to nature were inevitably seen to be—at the very least—interrupted by upper secondary and/or higher education. What the teachers in schools in the sparsely populated areas did to a greater degree than the teachers in schools of small de/industrialised communities was to establish a notion of the rural as something to be valued. In the larger schools there were few examples of the local context for global conditions, and few forms of interdependence were described where the local community was also actively contributing (Beach et al., 2019).

Even though education and school have been downplayed in this chapter (analyses of education and schools are made in other chapters in this book), the importance of the structuring of education for physical, social and mental attachments must be mentioned. Since choices of upper secondary education options did not exist or were limited in the local place, the 'learning to leave' discourse was self-evident and creating and developing sustainable platforms in order to maintain valued social, physical or mental attachments was difficult. This helps to confirm Corbett's (2007) and Forsey's (2015) insights regarding the messages schools send to non-academic and academic students alike regarding the desirability of moving beyond this place if you really want to get on.

Local events, sports and social media have been mentioned as possible means through which positive visions of the local place might be developed. However, none of these can be considered as durable in terms of developing notions of a rural idyll. No one mentioned sports to be a priority in keeping social relations healthy, neither those practising sports simply for fun nor those heading for the national team. Social media was often mentioned in interviews to be important for keeping in contact with local peers and for being updated by local bloggers. Since they claimed to interact locally with their social media usage, it could be argued that most of the young people interviewed related to their locality rather than the cosmopolitan or transregional. However, in classroom observations it was noted that electronic devices were actually used for many *non-local* things, for instance watching videos on YouTube and doing online shopping. In fact, there were no sustainable examples of what Appadurai (1995) refers to as producing locality.

The use of social media use can, of course, take place anywhere, and it might have been different if some of these adolescents lived closer to each other—then the distance would not have been an issue. It is often argued that social media offers the possibility of interacting without the restrictions imposed by place and distance. However, few of the youths participating in this project used this possibility. And it cannot be convincingly argued either that they used social media to produce a community based on a shared and distinctively local ideology. In short, electronic mediation was not really used to produce or share many of the youths' positive visions of their place or to counter the power geometry of the centre.

It is outside the scope of this research to see if local chat groups or Facebook groups persisted when the young people moved elsewhere to further their education, and if they did persist the effects on the young people's feelings of attachment to their local place. The consumption of media, other than that which was locally produced, most probably contributed to a cosmopolitan understanding of self, but it was not apparent in the material other than in the classroom observations mentioned above. Local interactions through sports and social media fell short when the young people talked about their future (i.e. silences, not mentioned, see further chapter four). Those not aiming for a national team said that they would finish their sport when moving to upper secondary school, while for those aiming at national team representation their local peers were not seen as important for their advancement.

Discussion

Differences between the research sites are important and will be discussed at length in later chapters. For the purposes of the argument here, however, it is important to note that the most prominent difference was between the sparsely populated areas and the de/industrialised communities. Among the students in the three thinly populated regions, physical, social and mental attachments came out in different ways, as, for example, during talk of owning a family mountain cabin, discussions of the value of natural resources and a more emphasised notion of a rural idyll. However, young people from these same areas also formulated a strong critique that cited the harshness of living in rural areas, such as the difficulties imposed by distance and isolation and limited economic resources. And although most students claimed that everyone knew everyone and that this was largely a good thing, this was only partially true: on closer inspection it turned out that everyone did not know everyone, and the idea of using those tightknit connections which did exist to assert influence and get things done did not seem to have occurred to the interviewees.

Even though it can be argued that each individual rural youth in this study represents a unique case which comprises several place-related identities depending on the context of the observation or interview topic, some recurring themes can be identified. Our feeling is that the suggestion (Vertovec and Cohen, 2002) of a cosmopolitan youth culture where the youth is seen as independent of the local and unlimited within the global can be questioned in relation to youth living in rural contexts. *The local*, in the form of physical and social resources and mental attachment, seemed important and valued by most of the young people we spoke to. Nevertheless, they were not unaffected by dominant discourses of cosmopolitanism and hegemonic individualism (the effects were most prominent in thoughts on future careers, see chapter four). The residential preferences of rural youths can be regarded as the outcome of a complex relationship with their surroundings, since cosmopolitan living does not seem to attract them more than the lack of resources in a rural context pushes them away. The dominant discourses, and for most the self-evident truth that their future will take place elsewhere, seemed to make it difficult for them to collectively gather information that would strengthen their identity as defined by place (see further discussions chapter four on future careers).

Many of the adolescents in this project seem to struggle with the question of belonging to a *good* place. In their view they already live in a *good* place where they share valued social *spaces* (cf. Sørensen and Pless, 2017). In terms of social spaces young people seem to struggle with the same question, as is well-known from research on urban youth (Reay and Lucey, 2000; Bunar and Ambrose, 2016). Even though rural youth know their place to be widely stigmatised for having fewer options, they have developed social relations and spaces which they value and do not want to give up. They discuss different ways to maintain things but the possibility of staying is in most cases not seen as an option. Even though there were some who distanced themselves from the place they lived and the social spaces related to it, most of the rural youth expressed more ambivalence and equivocation. They shared a sense of belonging, but one which was undercut by the lack of wider recognition of the rural as something to be valued; the virtues of rural life have largely been silenced by the deafening hegemonic discourses on individualism (independence of others) and cosmopolitanism (independence of place). Presented representations certainly question (as Jamison (2000 p. 203) argues) 'Baumanesque *late modernist* sociological theorising', which sees individuals as disembedded from place. Or as Massey puts it: 'There is a need to face up to—rather than simply deny—people's need for attachment of some sort...' (Massey, 1994, p. 151). However, it seems that there is little the young people do, or indeed can do, to challenge the strong discourses in the media and among politicians that devalue rural places as cherished physical, social and mental spaces important to the youth.

References

Appadurai, A. (1995) The production of locality, in Fardon, R. (ed), *Counterworks: Managing the diversity of knowledge*, London: Routledge.

Beach, D., Johansson, M., Öhrn, E., Rönnlund, M. and Rosvall, P.-Å. (2019) Rurality and education relations: Metro-centricity and local values in rural communities and rural schools; *European Educational Research Journal*, 18(1): 19-33.

Bevelander, P. and Pendakur, R. (2014) The labour market integration of refugee and family reunion immigrants: a comparison of outcomes in Canada and Sweden, *Journal of Ethnic and Migration Studies*, 40(5): 689-709.

Bunar, N. and Ambrose, A. (2016) Schools, choice and reputation: Local school markets and the distribution of symbolic capital in segregated cities, *Research in Comparative and International Education*, 11(1): 34-51.

Cedering, M. (2016) *Konsekvenser av skolnedläggningar [Consequences of school closures]*, Uppsala: Uppsala University.

Corbett, M. (2005) Rural education and out-migration: The case of a coastal community, *Canadian journal of education*, 28(1-2): 52-72.

Corbett, M. (2007) *Learning to leave: The irony of schooling in a costal community*, Halifax: Fernwood publishing.

Corbett, M. (2013) I'm going to make sure I'm ready before I leave: The complexity of educational and mobility decision-making in a Canadian coastal community. *Journal of Rural Studies*, 32: 275-282.

Forsey, M. (2015) Learning to Stay? Mobile Modernity and the Sociology of Choice. *Mobilities*, 10(5): 764-783.

Gordon, T., Holland, J. and Lahelma, E. (2000) *Making Spaces: Citizenship and Difference in Schools*, Houndmills: MacMillan Press LTD.

Halfacree, K. H. (1995) Talking about rurality: Social representations of the rural as expressed by residents of six English parishes, *Journal of Rural Studies*, 11(1): 1-20.

Jamieson, L. (2000) Migration, Place and Class: Youth in a Rural Area, *The Sociological Review*, 48(2): 203-223.

Johansson, M. (2017) "Yes, the power is in the town": An ethnographic study of student participation in a rural Swedish secondary school, *Australian and International journal of rural education*, 27(2): 61-77.

Krivokapic-Skoko, B. and Collins, J. (2016) Looking for Rural Idyll 'Down Under': International Immigrants in Rural Australia, *International Migration*, 54(1): 167-179.

Leyshon, M. (2008) The betweeness of being a rural youth: inclusive and exclusive lifestyles, *Social and Cultural Geography*, 9(1): 1-26.

Massey, D. (1994) *Space, place and gender*, Cambridge: Polity press.

Matthews, H., Taylor, M., Sherwood, K., Tucker, F. and Melanie, L. (2000) Growing-up in the countryside: children and the rural idyll. *Journal of Rural Studies*, 16(2): 141-153.

Moskal, M. (2015) 'When I think home I think family here and there': Translocal and social ideas of home in narratives of migrant children and young people, *Geoforum*, 58: 143-152.

Paulgaard, G. (2017) Geographies of inequalities in an area of opportunities: ambiguous experiences among young men in the Norwegian High North, *Geographical Research*, 55(1): 38-46.

Reay, D. and Lucey, H. (2000) 'I Don't Really like It Here but I Don't Want to Be Anywhere Else': Children and Inner City Council Estates, *Antipode*, 32(4): 410-428.

Rönnlund, M. (2019) I love this place, but I won't stay'. Identification with place and imagined spatial futures amongst youth living in rural areas in Sweden, *Young*, online first.

Rönnlund, M., Rosvall, P.-Å. and Johansson, M. (2018) Vocational or academic track? Study and career plans among Swedish students living in rural areas, *Journal of Youth Studies*, 21(3): 360-375.

Rosvall, P.-Å. (2017) Understanding career development amongst immigrant youth in a rural place, *Intercultural Education*, 28(6): 523-542.

Rye, J. F. (2006) Rural youths' images of the rural, *Journal of Rural Studies*, 22(4): 409-421.

Smith, D. P. and Higley, R. (2012) Circuits of education, rural gentrification, and family migration from the global city, *Journal of Rural Studies*, 28(1): 49-55.

Stenbacka, S. (2016) International migration and resilience: Rural introductory spaces and refugee immigration as a resource, in Tamásy, C. and Revilla Diez, J. (eds), *Regional resilience, economy and society: Globalising rural places*, Oxon: Routledge.

Svendsen, G. L. H. and Svendsen, G. T. (2016) Homo voluntarius and the rural idyll: Voluntary work, trust and solidarity in rural and urban areas, *The Journal of Rural and Community Development*, 11(1): 56-72.

Sørensen, N. U. and Pless, M. (2017) Living on the Periphery of Youth:Young People's Narratives of Youth Life in Rural Areas, *Young*, 25(4suppl): 1-17.

Waldron, J. (1992) Minority cultures and the cosmopolitan alternative, *University of Michigan Journal of Law reform*, 25(1): 751-793.

Valentine, G. (1997) A safe place to grow up? Parenting, perceptions of children's safety and the rural idyll, *Journal of Rural Studies*, 13(2): 137-148.

Vertovec, S. and Cohen, R. (2002) Introduction: Conceiving cosmopolitanism, in Vertovec, S. and Cohen, R. (eds), *Conceiving cosmopolitanism*. Oxford: Oxford University Press.

Youdell, D. (2004) Engineering school markets, constituting schools and subjectivating students: the bureaucratic, institutional and classroom dimensions of educational triage, *Journal of Education Policy*, 19(4): 407-431.

Åberg-Bengtsson, L. (2009) The smaller the better? A review of research on small rural schools in Sweden, *International Journal of Educational Research*, 48(2): 100-108.

Chapter 3

The local place in the pedagogic practices

Per-Åke Rosvall

Introduction

The analysis presented in this chapter focuses on the presence of *the local*, understood as the local place, its surroundings and social interactions, within the pedagogic practices in the researched schools. Students' and teachers' talk about the local place's presence in the pedagogic practices is also analysed, as well as silences about the local place in student talk and teaching. Attention is paid to the local place in general, but particularly use of the local as individual enhancement, social inclusion and political participation (see further explanation below).

Like other researchers (Arnot and Reay, 2004; McLean, Abbas, and Ashwin, 2013), to analyse civic and critical education we have applied Bernstein's concepts of pedagogic rights. They are used in combination with the more overarching theoretical concepts of Massey (1994) that provided key parts of the theoretical framework for the project, as outlined in chapter one. Unlike Massey's constructs, Bernsteinian theory specifically applies to education. Thus combining Massey's and Bernstein's concepts seems useful for acquiring deeper understandings. According to Bernstein, the first pedagogic right, individual enhancement, is 'the means of critical understanding and to seeing new possibilities' and access to it expands personal horizons, resulting in *confidence* (Bernstein, 2000, p. xx). The second pedagogic right, social inclusion, is 'to be included socially, intellectually, culturally and personally [including] the right [to be] autonomous' (Bernstein, 2000, p. xx), and results in a sense of belonging. Civic education illuminates the interaction between individuals and social systems or structure. This knowledge allows students to gain insight into and ask questions about why people, including themselves, are as they are. The third pedagogic right is political participation "in the construction, maintenance and transformation of social order' (Bernstein, 2000, p xxi). The pedagogic rights are analysed by using the concepts of classification and framing (Bernstein, 1990, 2000). Classification concerns 'relations between categories' (2000 p. 6), particularly here the degrees to which local interactions, systems and structures are classified as important in relation to those at regional, national or global levels. 'Framing refers to the nature of the control over: the selection of communication; its sequencing; its pacing; the criteria; and the control over the social base which makes this transmission possible' (2000 p. 12-13). Where framing is strong, the transmitter controls the selection etc. Where the framing is weak, the acquirer controls the selection. Pertinent examples here include the degree to which locally produced material is used together with national textbooks and local settings or events (particularly any highlighted as meaningful by students) are used as teaching opportunities. Classification and framing are analytical concepts and thus not separable in the pedagogic practice. However, they are powerful concepts for analysing what hinders or facilitates what Bernstein describes as pedagogic rights.

Various researchers have noted that workbooks used in school mostly cover content related to the capital of the state and the middle and upper classes (Davies, Evans, and Reid, 2005; Lingard and Mills, 2007; Hoadley, 2008;). This can be understood, and has been criticised, as knowledge or content centrism in pedagogic practices. For example, researchers for years have criticised history course books for devoting too much attention to the history of wars and kings, while seldom portraying local history and histories of the working classes (Hawkey, 2015; Van Straaten, Wilschut, and Oostdam, 2016) or women (Ohlander, 2010). A counter argument is that such centrism provides a common hierarchical framework, enabling everyone within a nation, region or the world to develop a shared understanding of relevant events and processes. However, educational researchers have also raised didactical reasons to include more local content, in addition to the important hierarchical dimension that comes with focusing on more central affairs (cf. Bernstein's pedagogic rights). They argue that generic understandings can be more easily fostered by referring to the individual learner's own circumstances and experiences. Therefore, such researchers stress the importance of balancing factual knowledge and knowledge without a given answer (Odenstad, 2010; Christensen, 2013), as well as the specific and generic (Sandalh, 2015). In other words it seems easier to problematise global issues and conflicts in the world if you can relate them to issues and conflicts in your own local place. Thus, it is important to analyse the degree to which the local features in pedagogic practices and content, if and how the local is related to broader contexts, as well as students' and teachers' thoughts about its inclusion. This chapter contributes to such analysis by presenting and discussing relevant observations in the six researched schools.

Results

In this section, observed classroom activities and content are analysed as well as observations of sport days, thematic days, visits, work place learning and career counselling. To cover what was included about the local, and how it was valued, the chapter is divided into two parts. The first part describes the local's inclusion in pedagogic practices and content, both generally and more specifically in relation to critical civic education. The second part initially considers students' thoughts and then teachers' thoughts, as expressed in their recorded talk. The analytical work is foremost made by me, but the analytical work has been shared in project meetings throughout the writing process. It is based on the material from all the six schools collected by the three field researchers in the project group.

Pedagogic practices in general

When project group examined all the collected empirical material all researchers noted a substantial difference in the local's inclusion in the pedagogic practices and content between the three schools in sparsely populated areas and the three in de/industrialised communities. In the three sparsely populated areas the local place was much more commonly referred to in the classroom tasks and talk. In addition, their sports or thematic days were more frequently connected to local historical events or points of interest. Local practices or events were also more frequently raised spontaneously, as in the following observations:

> Monica calls the teacher's attention and asks how to do the task. The teacher kneels down and says: "Think of two individuals that live in different places, one in Stockholm and one 50 kilometres outside Mountain. Both need to use their cars to commute to their work" [continuing to explain the task].   (Mountain School, October 19)

The local place was not only spontaneously raised, as in this excerpt, but also used in planned activities. For example, in Mountain School, the history teacher discussed how the Second World War had affected the community, in terms of political and economic insecurity, refugees, loyalties (risks of being called a traitor if you hosted refugees or confessed to supporting the 'wrong side'). The teacher also took an opportunity to further explore these issues when the class visited the local museum. The teacher summarised the visit in the next lesson, and connected local events during the Second World War to recent local phenomena:

The teacher summarises the visit to the museum and says that the war affected quite a lot of people although Sweden was never officially engaged. The teacher mentions the old woman who was imprisoned by the Nazis and Mountain's physician who helped refugees from different nations who had made it across the Norwegian border and escaped to Mountain. Many of the refugees were quite ill because they had endured harsh conditions during their escape. The teacher then turns to the recent arrival of quite a few refugee immigrants in Mountain. The teacher stresses that the refugees should be treated with the same respect that the doctor had treated refugees during the Second World War.

(Mountain School, October 23)

In this and similar cases the local place and local events were clearly classified as important, and local facilities (here the local museum) were used in framing of tasks. By placing a major global event in the local context, the teacher (and the museum's instructor) showed the importance of the local and the global significance of local events, and vice versa. In an interesting comparison, the Second World War theme was also covered during the field observations by the class at River School (one of the schools in the de/industrialised communities where the local was rarely included in pedagogic practice and content). During the observation period River's connections to the Second World War were not mentioned at all. It was primarily treated as a European event and the Swedish neutrality was highlighted. It could be argued that River was situated further from national borders and its community had less direct exposure to human consequences of the war than the people in Mountain. However, during the observation period there were exhibitions of texts, postcards and pictures from a local refugee camp in the local library (not the school library), and similar documentation of an event in which the Norwegian military hosted the community at the railway station during the war. Thus, illustrations of local people's exposure to wider events during the war were publicly displayed in the local community, but they did not seem to be classified as important in teaching.

In four of the schools there were students who had at least one parent of Sámi background. Sámi people are indigenous groups with similar culture and ethnicity, who live mostly in northern parts of Sweden, Norway and Finland. They were originally nomadic, but today most Sámi people do not practice a nomadic life at all, or only to a limited extent. However, there have been various efforts to increase the population (and extraction of resources) in the region since the 16th century, when king Gustav Vasa encouraged settlement in the north by, *inter alia*, reducing taxes for people who voluntarily migrated from southern parts of the country. Rapid industrialisation in the 19th century and associated increases in demand for wood triggered further surges in immigration and exploitation of resources, accompanied by conflicts between new settlers and Sámi people, with increasing regulation of Sámi people's activities (Lantto, 2014). Nevertheless, contentious issues associated with recognition of Sámi people, their democratic rights, and conflicts between domiciled and Sámi people, and between Sámi people and the state, have still not been resolved. Pedagogic content related to Sámi culture was recorded in the four schools situated in the north. This was observed most frequently in Mountain School (where the monitored class had Sámi-related content in Home economics, Crafts, English and German courses) and least frequently in River School, where observed Sámi-related content was restricted to the class making Sámi-inspired knifes in Crafts lessons. In three of the four schools the students did craftwork associated with Sámi culture, and this was described as an important element of the students' crafts education by teachers:

> While the students work on their tasks I ask the teacher if the students are often allowed to do tin embroidery [a typically Sámi craft]. She says yes, and since I knew she was from southern Sweden I asked if it was common there too. Then she said: 'Not at all! And it was not included in my crafts education there. But when I knew I'd be staying here I took a course in [Sámi] tin embroidery. I wanted to learn. We have students with Sámi background.' (Inland School, October 7)

Thus, there were several examples of representation of the local in the observed practices. There were also some examples of the students going out and using nature as a resource to learn more about the local. For instance, the students in Inland School visited a local national park and were assigned tasks related to National Parks in several subsequent lessons:

> As a final written account of the work, the students are supposed to write an essay discussing why National Parks are important and what makes particular National Parks special […]. They were given a booklet with information about National Parks and … the National Park they visited

> together with a long recently published article about the National Park from a local newspaper. (Inland School, October 14)

In Forest School, no substantial thematic work connected to local surroundings during lessons was observed in the field studies, but connections were drawn to various aspects of the local community and nature. For example, when the students were constructing models in Technology the teacher stressed the importance of coping with pressure from a lot of snow.

> The students are working in two divided groups (…). In Technology the students are working on various constructions that include hydraulic systems, e.g. movable bridges. The teachers say that it is important for the constructions to be able to withstand pressure from a lot of snow. (Forest School, April 21)

In such respects, the local natural environment was a compulsory component of the curriculum and the teacher emphasised the importance of highlighting favourable aspects of local features and conditions. There were also examples of not only school staff but also other members of the local community contributing to the school events. For example, in Forest School a sports day ended with a dinner that locals had contributed to:

> This day ends with a big banquet where the students are supposed to be well dressed. Good food is provided, including some contributed by the local hunters (meat from moose they had hunted). (Forest School, March 27)

The examples above are from Mountain, Inland and Forest Schools. These are the schools in the sparsely populated areas, and it was in these areas that the local most commonly and prominently featured in the pedagogic practices and content. In some cases the local was also used in River, Sea and Coast Schools, but less frequently. In Coast School, for example, there were no observed cases in the classroom context, but one in an excursion, when the students wandered along a path of historical importance and the local history there was acknowledged. Thus, there was not complete silence about local history or matters in any of the schools, but all three field researchers noted a difference in this respect between the schools in the sparsely populated areas and those in the de/industrialised communities. In the schools in the sparsely populated areas, content concerning the local place arose both in spontaneous and planned forms. Moreover, spontaneous content raised by both teachers and students, through articulations about local experiences, was treated as important by teachers and in most cases included in the theme. In ordinary classroom activities this was most prominent when cultural themes were addressed in Crafts lessons. However, it was also common in sport days, thematic days (historic walks or outdoor education) and visits.

Pedagogic practices related to critical civic education

As shown in the previous section, in the three sparsely populated areas (Mountain, Inland and Forest) the local place was mentioned and pedagogic practices were related to local events, culture, business and activities quite often. In most of those occurrences of the local in the pedagogic practices, the local was treated in a quite neutral fashion or romanticised. For example, when activities such as reindeer herding by indigenous people and timber rafting were covered as pedagogic content, the hard, hazardous work involved was usually downplayed in relation to the romantic elements of working close to nature. In the following excerpt, conflicts following establishment of a hydropower plant to exploit the local river is not mentioned, although it had severe consequences:

> The group gathers outside the classroom and the teacher tells us that we are going to the power plant on the river and watch when the salmon are spawning. /... / We have a first stop on a bridge where there is an information board and a *fish ladder* for the salmon. The teacher describes what happened to the salmon when the power plant was built—the salmon almost disappeared. (Sea School, October 15)

It should be mentioned that the teacher presented the building of the power plant and near-disappearance of salmon with a tone and body posture that could be understood as critical, but did not verbalise or further comment on the critique. In such cases, there was an apparent discrepancy with the following statements in the Swedish curriculum (Lgy, 2011):

The goals of the school are that each student:
- can consciously determine and express ethical standpoints based on knowledge of human rights and basic democratic values, as well as personal experiences [...]

Teachers should:
* openly communicate and discuss different values, views and problems (p. 14-15)

In addition, School staff should:
* in the education take advantage of contacts in the local community, through its organisations in working and cultural life [in addition to other mentioned local and personal resources]. (p. 12).

In our observations, local events and the students' own local personal experiences were seldom used to express ethical standpoints or democratic values, but according to the interviewed students there was no shortage of such examples. These included conflicts with immigrants mentioned by students in River, Forest, Sea and Mountain Schools. School seemed to be a neutral place, and conflicts occurred after school and elsewhere, but they were well known to teachers and heads at the schools. For example, during the observation period at Mountain School threats were posted in social media to burn down a local hostel for refugees. The incident was covered by regional media, and the staff were so concerned about the incident that the head visited all the classes and informed them that it would be an unacceptable crime. Although the perpetrator was not known, the incident was talked about as being done by someone outside school. Moreover, when the teachers followed up the head's visit it was not used to 'openly communicate and discuss different values, views and problems'. None of the interviewed students said that physical actions against immigrants were acceptable, but several boys said they thought that numbers of immigrants should be restricted. However, local conflicts or the students' own experiences of immigrants, immigration or racism were seldom used in the pedagogic practices as planned content. On a few occasions questions concerning immigrants arose spontaneously, as illustrated by this excerpt from Inland:

> The students are preparing for a visit to the local municipality administration and politicians, which is a part of a group work activity on the municipalities duties. One of the groups immediately starts to talk about the refugee immigrants in Inland. Jack says: "Now there are 300 immigrants here. You can only guess how much that costs. I think that's wrong! Them getting clothes, food and all that. And I don't think the municipality should pay a private company for housing them." A girl answers: "But think again. They can't stay in their own countries. Would you like to be there? We need to take care of them." The teacher circulates

'The local place' in the pedagogic practices 53

in the classroom and comes to the group. The teacher raises her voice and says: "It's not the decision of the municipality to accept immigrants. The municipality needs to provide places for them to live and schooling. Since the municipality does not have housing of its own, we're dependent on private solutions. But never mind that. Get back to your task."

(Inland School, November 3)

On the few occasions questions concerning immigrants arose spontaneously, the teachers acknowledged the students' concerns, but soon shifted the focus to other matters or downplayed the issues. In this excerpt, for example, the teacher points out that the municipality must meet some needs of immigrants (housing and schooling), but paradoxically says the students should return to questions concerning the municipality. What the teacher does is to classify content concerning immigrants as a taboo subject, and accentuates the classification by raising her voice.

However, neglecting or downplaying local conflicts generally and those with immigrants specifically is not restricted to rural education. Similar apparent reluctance to engage directly with the issues has been observed in city and urban schools too, indicating that teachers are often uncertain about how to handle immigration and racism as pedagogic content (Norberg, 2000; Beach, Dovemark, Schwartz, and Öhrn, 2013; Rosvall and Öhrn, 2014). Nevertheless, there was one exception both to the tendency for local issues to feature more frequently in the sparsely populated areas and the generally low engagement with immigrant issues. A young asylum-seeking immigrant in Sea School, one of the de-industrialised communities, attracted lots of support from students and teachers, as well as other members of the local community. Their action was not successful ultimately, and the immigrant was deported, but it was strongly symbolic. However, it should be noted that this incident involved (and focused attention on) a conflict between a group of individuals in the local community and national authorities, rather than conflicting views in the local community.

Thus, in terms of Bernstein's concepts, local conflicts were rarely (if ever) classified as important content: not only conflicts with (or about) immigrants but also other controversial issues and conflicts with other groups were neglected, avoided or downplayed. In particular, our empirical data show that conflicts involving Sámi people were not treated as important content, even though some of the students and teachers had a Sámi background. It may seem surprising that the students were not given opportunities to learn about and discuss historical and current conflicts, in terms that could foster understanding of local arguments and their origins. However, our data support other empirical findings that it seems difficult for teachers to address local conflicts, and thus are hesitant to include them in teaching content (Carretero, 2017). This is assumed to be at least partly because the conflicts are (or might be) infectious and discussions might easily get out of hand: as Bentrovato et al.,(2016) put it in their book *History Can Bite*. However, avoiding local events, some of which the students themselves will have experience of, arguably misses opportunities to use students' own experiences, which reportedly increases interest (Christensen, 2013; Sandalh, 2015). In addition, shifting between local and regional, national or global perspectives increases general understandings of matters (Davies et al., 2005). In terms of Bernstein's arguments, outlined above, avoiding local conflicts misses opportunities to foster the first pedagogic right: 'the means of critical understanding and to seeing new possibilities' and the resulting *confidence*. It also restricts the second pedagogic right: 'to be included socially, intellectually, culturally and personally' and students' possibility to gain insight into and ask questions about why people, including themselves, are as they are. Moreover, the pedagogic practices contribute little to the third pedagogic right, i.e. political participation 'in the construction, maintenance and transformation of social order'.

It is also noteworthy that hierarchical dimensions of who and what are represented identified in other research, i.e. the greater representation of the middle and upper classes than working classes, were also apparent in our observations. Working class interests, struggles, conflicts and events seemed to be downplayed. For example, during the observation period the students at one school were covering a historical era that included a well-known workers' demonstration, which can be considered a national landmark event and occurred just fifty kilometres away from the school. The event is the subject of several novels and referred to sometimes by reporters and politicians, generally as an example of state violation of fundamental democratic rights. It was cited in the Swedish parliament as recently as 2001 during debates about anti-terrorism laws following the 9/11 attacks on the World Trade Center in New York. However, the historical event was not mentioned by the teacher during coverage of the time period. A similar pattern was observed in representation of individuals. For example, during activities on local history and culture, none of the timber rafting workers or indigenous people were mentioned by name. During the observed events, individuals mentioned by name as important for the local community were usually middle- to upper-class or wealthy people such as doctors and foundry proprietors. Workers' contributions and political rights were ignored.

Students' and teachers' thoughts about the local in pedagogic practices

The inclusion of local practices and students' (local) experiences is, as already mentioned, stipulated in the Swedish curriculum and researchers have highlighted its ability for increasing interest and improve learning outcomes. Thus, it is interesting to analyse how students and teachers discussed what was and was not included about their local place and local events in the pedagogic practices.

Students' thoughts

Most students said in the interviews that it was interesting to know more about what had happened, what was happening and effects of events in their local community and its surroundings:

> It is interesting to know how Inland came about and why, although I'm not that interested in history and such things. Still, it's interesting that it grew from a tiny village round a church into a small community.
> (Inland School, October 14)

However, responses seemed to differ somewhat between students in classes where local content was included rarely and those in classes where it was included relatively often. Students in the class followed in River School, where little local content was included, were interested in learning more about their local place but seemed to have problems articulating what that might entail:

Interviewer: In the classes I've been, the local place and what has happened and is happening here now has only been mentioned a few times. For example, the mathematics teacher asked you to use local examples from the local supermarkets when you calculated costs for food. Do you have any thoughts about that?
Rolf: Yes, ehh, I think it would be very interesting to learn more about what happened here.
Interviewer: In history you learned about the Second World War. Do you know what happened here then?

Robert: No. But that would also be very interesting.
(River School, April 22)

Students in Mountain School (where the local was more frequently included in the pedagogic practices) also favoured more local content. For example, most of the Mountain School students thought of the local as both interesting and important, as manifested by comments such as 'I didn't know that it happened here, it was really interesting to know' and 'It's easier to understand when you can relate things to your own place'. However, they also criticised the content currently included, because they thought some themes recurred over and over again:

> It's him all the time, we've heard about him since preschool. This time at the museum there were a few new things that I didn't know about him that were interesting, but it's him all the time.
> (Mountain School, November 10)

Sometimes they also critisised the field researchers' understandings of *local*:

Interviewer: What do you think about the thematic days with local cultural events you had?

Mona: They're good fun and interesting, but they're not about us. Those who arrange comes from other places nearby and [large town at the coast] and their customs are not really like ours. For example we don't make [local dish] like they do.
(Mountain School, November 12)

Including the local in pedagogic content also seemed to raise the students' awareness of what they thought of as relevant content, and what was considered local or not. However, the students were not democratically involved in choosing content, what should be classified as relevant or interesting, or how this content should be framed. So, their critique could not be formalised in order to change content or practices. In Bernstein's words it seemed that training in dealing with local issues fostered individual enhancement (and hence pedagogic rights) through provision of means for critical understanding and expansion of personal horizons.

'The local place' in the pedagogic practices

All students were asked what they thought about using events or issues derived from the local place in the pedagogic practice, including observed themes, other themes and generally. Interestingly, not only native students but also those with an immigrant background stressed its importance:

Interviewer: In the classes I've been, the local place and what happened and happens here has been mentioned, for example when you had classes on the Second World War and thematic work on indigenous people. Do you have any thoughts about that?
Majid: Yes, it's very interesting!
Interviewer: What do you find interesting?
Majid: It's interesting to learn more about the local place where you live.
Interviewer: Sorry for being blunt, but you said earlier that you were brought up in [a multimillion town in Asia] and that you'll probably move after 9th grade [a few months after the interview]. Why is it interesting to learn more about Mountain?
Majid: Because it's here that I live now. It's important to know things about the places you lived. And things gets more real when you know where they took place. (Mountain School, December 12)

A question asked by Virta (2016) in relation to her research, 'Whose history should be dealt with in a pluricultural context?' is also relevant to the above excerpt. Virta is mostly concerned about teaching national history in a pluricultural context and the question might be even more poignant when including the relevance of the local context. Majid responded quite simply and frankly to that question:

It's important to include both. (Mountain School, December 12)

Following Majid's suggestion, the pedagogic practice should include, or in Bernstein's terms classify, history or events of places where the students live and where they have lived as important content (cf. Harris and Reynolds, 2014; Nordgren, 2017). Massey (1994) argues that globalisation is taking place somewhere and, with immigrants in the classroom, globalisation in terms of transnationalism is highly visible. These, and various other authors, as well as the Swedish curriculum (Lgy, 2011), strongly recommend inclusion and problematisation of students' local experience. Thus, there is robust support for

Majid's argument. Given the possibility for students to learn from their own (local) experiences, which are increasingly global, it seems important to include content that problematises the local in relation to the global and vice versa.

Teachers' thoughts

As shown above there were substantial differences in degrees of inclusion of local content in the observed pedagogy, particularly between the three sparsely populated areas and three de/industrialised communities (see also chapter two). It is difficult to identify cause and effect in this context. However, classification and contextual analysis of the local's inclusion in teaching content in the schools in sparsely populated areas revealed that it was often linked to power relations with 'the outside'. 'The power's in the town' was a commonly expressed notion (cf. Johansson, 2017), often in combination with 'They don't understand our situation' or 'It's important to know cultures or politics of the cities'. As one teacher put it:

> I've lived long enough in different places to know that you're not less prepared for life just because you were brought up in a rural area. I'm very tired of urban values being taken as norms and schools being seen as better just because they have more students'
>
> (Mountain School, December 3)

Although the local seemed to be included more in practices of the three schools in sparsely populated areas, there was strong classification of various local events and issues as relevant or (apparently) irrelevant even in these schools. As shown above, critical content related to indigenous people and immigrants was avoided, but some more neutral content was also considered insufficiently relevant, even when desires to include it were expressed:

> When I was talking with the principal, he said there are strong desires to include hunting in the school's schedule (schemat) and that as principal he is not popular when he says that hunting is not part of the students' education. (Forest School, May 4)

In the de/industrialised communities, where the local was rarely mentioned or included in pedagogic content and practices, interviewed teachers did not seem to have thought about the possibility very much:

> *Interviewer:* Have you thought of including more work on River in your tasks?
>
> *Teacher, history:* I haven't. But now you ask me about it, it seems worthwhile. For example in Geography tasks I use Google maps and it's always difficult to make them listen before they've found their own house. Starting with River might be a possibility to gain interest.
>
> (River School, April 22)

Moreover, the local did not seem to be on River School's agenda since none of the teachers, the head, or other staff (librarians etc.) seem to have raised it as an important issue. However, this does not explain the difference in its inclusion between the schools in sparsely populated areas and de/industrialised communities, because (for example) the greater inclusion of the local in Inland School was not apparently due to an agenda articulated by the school's head. Indeed, the head's responses during an interview indicate a lack of awareness of the matter, and apparent belief that appropriate inclusion of the local will occur without clear articulation:

> It's more about the local place from first to sixth grade [age 7-12]. Here, in seventh to ninth grade we don't have any particular focus on the local, except when we work with the local labour market. However, I think that the local is brought up anyway. The teachers who work here live here as well. If somethings happens in Inland everyone talks about it.
>
> (Inland School, October 14)

These observations indicate that provision of pedagogic rights, as described by Bernstein, may require of a more articulated agenda regarding the relations between democratic values and personal [local] experiences as presented and accessed via the schools' pedagogic contents and practices. In this respect it may be illuminating to repeat Bernstein's words:'

> How a society selects, classifies, distributes, transmits and evaluates the educational knowledge it considers to be public, reflects both the distribution of power and principles of social control.
>
> (Bernstein, 1971 p. 202)

This is reflected in a stark contrast between the schools highlighted above. The local was not on agendas of either River or Inland Schools, while in Mountain School it featured in planned teaching content and/or teachers raised aspects of the local place spontaneously, and politicians actively promoted inclusion of local content in the teaching practices:

> *Teacher, social science*: My daughter-in-law works as a museum instructor. She used to be a teacher, teaching grades 4 to 6. But when the municipality decided to invest in a full-time instructor at the museum she took some courses and got the position.
> (Mountain School, May 18)

Despite Mountain being a small municipality with a small budget for social services, politicians clearly seemed to think the local was important. However, there were also other important factors influencing teachers' interest in including local matters, for example their schools' geographic positions. Mountain is in a remote location, at the end of a road, which makes it difficult to commute. River, in contrast, is also rural but it has road links to some larger towns. Thus, River School has attracted young teachers who lacked sufficient experience to compete for positions in the surrounding towns. For instance, during the observation period the River School class had two newly qualified teachers who thought the school would be a good place to gain enough experience to compete for positions in nearby towns. They did not feel like *country people* (Campbell and Yates, 2011) and thus were not very concerned about *local matters*. In contrast, the head in Inland School mentioned the teachers' local attachment as a possible reason for coverage of the local despite its absence in any articulated agenda.

Discussion

A general conclusion from our research is that if pedagogic practices are to provide students with tools for construction, maintenance and transformation of social order, educational curricula must address notions of educational identity and agency in relation to the broad issues of classification, framing and power. That is, schools, communities and their power relations must be contextualised within the local, regional and global places, including rural-urban distinctions. Such needs to consider power relations have been noted in poor urban areas (Raffo, 2011). Our results corroborate the need and indicate that it extends to rural curricula. Within the six schools, the importance of including knowledge of local events and issues was differently classified, thus there were substantial differences in inclusion of the local in pedagogic content and practices among them. Productive pedagogies 'work together a politics of redistribution and politics of recognition politics' in a desire to maximise teachers' effects in terms of both knowledge production and formation of identity and disposition (Lingard, 2007). However, only one of the researched schools seemed to have a political agenda to include the local place in pedagogic content, which (of course) provides a more stable platform for classifying the local place as important content.

Our results show that the local place was more commonly classified as important pedagogic content in the three schools in sparsely populated areas. Thus, political classification and framing are not the only factors affecting inclusion of the local in pedagogic content. However, in a political era of marketisation of social services such as health care and education, which has inevitably led to metrocentricity in education and labour markets, it seems to be increasingly important to highlight the values of local places in sparsely populated areas. Both students and teachers in these areas referred to important aspects of their local places. This also occurred in the three de/industrialised communities, but not in the same articulated way. Inclusion of the local in pedagogic practices in the sparsely populated areas also seemed to enable the students to formulate critiques, positive and negative, of what was included.

The heads also indicated that teachers' local attachment, i.e. living in the area, was important for recognition of the local's importance. That seems to be correct, but some teachers in River had lived in River all their lives, except during some of their education and teacher training, but did not include the local in pedagogic content. Other important factors seem to include communities' sizes and geographic positions, and the political agenda. The agenda's importance is manifested in framing of the activities when the local was classified as important content in the three schools in sparsely populated areas, where it was relatively often included. Forest School did not have an articulated political agenda, and the local place featured as content largely in sport days or thematic days outside school. In Mountain and Inland Schools, the local was also included in *ordinary* classroom activities to a greater extent. Mountain's political agenda included promotion of awareness of local issues by, inter alia, employing individuals to raise them in pedagogic practices. Inland had a head who expressed the importance of local issues, but the political agenda was not as formalised as in Mountain. Thus, the political agenda seems to make a difference in terms of what is included, i.e. when and where the local place is framed and classified as important content.

However, deeper scrutiny of the content in the three schools where the local place was most frequently classified and framed as important indicates that local content was more recognitive than transformative. If understandings of the local place are important and valued, which the students' interviews imply, we need to consider how local matters can be included in content that imposes higher intellectual demands than more or less merely affirming their presence. The pedagogies mapped in the research provided few opportunities for fostering understandings of construction, maintenance and transformation of social order due to the near-absence of the conflict dimension. As Lingard (2007 p. 262) puts it: 'As such, they do not prepare students for the globalised world of the present, nor do they work in socially just ways.', which can also be understood as a critique of the researched pedagogic practices from a Bernsteinian understanding of pedagogic rights.

Previous researchers have claimed that civic education has drifted too far towards globalisation and/or cosmopolitanism, so students' experiences from their own everyday lives receive too little attention (Davies et al., 2005). The examples presented here, including comments by immigrants, clearly confirm that globalisation takes place somewhere and students feel that local matters should be discussed more often. However, the local needs to be related to the global, and the global to the local. It could be argued that education often builds on a dualistic discourse, for example manual-mental, sacred-profane, instruction-regulation, but really there is only one discourse, since discourses treated separately are intertwined. The same might be acknowledged in education for the distinction of the local and the global. Similarly, the distinction between the local and global may be artificial, although we observed few cases of the local and global being treated as intertwined. Thus, a suitable way to end this chapter may be to repeat Majid's simple statement above: 'It is important to include both.'

References

Arnot, M., and Reay, D. (2004) The framing of pedagogic encounters: Regulating the social order in classroom learning, in Muller, J. Davies, B. and Morais, A. (eds.) *Reading Bernstein, Researching Bernstein*. London: RoutledgeFalmer.

Beach, D., Dovemark, M., Schwartz, A., and Öhrn, E. (2013) Complexities and Contradictions of Educational Inclusion—A Meta-Ethnographic Analysis, *Nordic Studies in Education,* 33(04): 254-268.

Bentrovato, D., Korostelina, K., and Schulze, M. (2016) *History can bite: History education in divided and postwar societies*, Göttingen: V and R unipress.

Bernstein, B. (1971) *Class, codes and control. Volume I, Theoretical studies towards a sociology of language* (Vol. 1), Oxon: Routledge.
Bernstein, B. (1990) *Class, Codes and Control. Volume IV, The Structuring of Pedagogic Discourse*, Oxon: Routledge.
Bernstein, B. (2000) *Pedagogy, symbolic control and identity*, Lanham: Rowman and Littlefield Publishers.
Campbell, A., and Yates, G. (2011) Want to be a country teacher? No, I am too metrocentric, *Journal of Research in Rural Education*, 26(4): 1-12.
Carretero, M. (2017) The Teaching of Recent and Violent Conflicts as Challenges for History Education, in Psaltis, C., Carretero, M. and Čehajić-Clancy, S. (eds.) *History Education and Conflict Transformation: Social Psychological Theories, History Teaching and Reconciliation*, Cham: Springer International Publishing.
Christensen, T. (2013) Interdisciplinarity and self-reflection in civic education, *Nordidactica*, 3(1): 201-226.
Davies, I., Evans, M., and Reid, A. (2005) Globalising citizenship education? A critique of 'global education' and 'citzenship education', *British Journal of Educational Studies*, 53(1): 66-89.
Harris, R., and Reynolds, R. (2014) The history curriculum and its personal connection to students from minority ethnic backgrounds, *Journal of Curriculum Studies*, 46(4): 464-486.
Hawkey, K. (2015) Whose history is this anyway? Social justice and a history curriculum, *Education, Citizenship and Social Justice*, 10(3): 187-198.
Hoadley, U. (2008) Social class and pedagogy: a model for the investigation of pedagogic variation, *British Journal of Sociology of Education*, 29(1): 63-78.
Johansson, M. (2017) "Yes, the power is in the town": An ethnographic study of student participation in a rural Swedish secondary school, *Australian and International journal of rural education*, 27(2): 61-77.
Lantto, P. (2014) The consequences of the state intervention: Forced relocations and sámi rights in Sweden, 1919-2012, *Journal of ethnology and folkloristics*, 8(2): 53-73.
Lgy. (2011), *Curriculum for the compulsory school, preschool class and the recreation centre, 2011*, Stockholm: The Swedish National Agency for Education.
Lingard, B. (2007) Pedagogies of indifference. *International Journal of Inclusive Education*, 11(3): 245-266.
Lingard, B., and Mills, M. (2007) Pedagogies making a difference: issues of social justice and inclusion. *International Journal of Inclusive Education*, 11(3): 233-244.
McLean, M., Abbas, A., and Ashwin, P. (2013) A Bernsteinian View of Learning and Teaching Undergraduate Sociology-based Social Science, *Enhancing Learning in the Social Sciences*, 5(2): 32-44.
Norberg, K. (2000) Intercultural education and teacher education in Sweden, *Teaching and Teacher Education*, 16(4): 511-519.
Nordgren, K. (2017) Powerful knowledge, intercultural learning and history education. *Journal of Curriculum Studies*, 49(5): 663-682.
Odenstad, C. (2010) *Prov och bedömning i samhällskunskap. En analys av gymnasielärares skriftliga prov*, Karlstad: Karlstad university press.
Ohlander, A.-S. (2010) *Kvinnor, män och jämställdhet i läromedel i historia: En granskning på uppdrag av Delegationen för jämställdhet i skolan: SOU 2010:10*, Stockholm: Fritzes.

Raffo, C. (2011) Educational Equity in Poor Urban Contexts—Exploring Issues of Place/Space and Young People's Identity and Agency, *British Journal of Educational Studies,* 59(1): 1-19.

Rosvall, P.-Å., and Öhrn, E. (2014) Teachers' silences about racist attitudes and students' desires to address these attitudes, *Intercultural Education,* 25(5): 337-348.

Sandalh, J. (2015) Preparing for citizenship: The value of second order concepts in social science education, *Journal of social science education,* 14(1): 19-30.

Van Straaten, D., Wilschut, A., and Oostdam, R. (2016) Making history relevant to students by connecting past, present and future: a framework for research, *Journal of Curriculum Studies, 48*(4): 479-502.

Virta, A. (2016) Whose history should be dealt with in a pluricultural context—immigrant adolescents' approach, *Intercultural Education,* 27(4): 377-387.

Chapter 4

Careers, agency and place. Rural students reflect on their future

Maria Rönnlund

Introduction

In this chapter the nature and significance of learning in young people's lives in relation to agency and place is attended to. Establishing a career path is seen as an integral part of the learning and living of all youth, but the chapter deals specifically with rural students' thoughts about their future studies and careers in these particular respects: What is it that appears to be important when individual students reflect on their futures in terms of study and career pathways? And what is the influence of gender, class relations and other structural factors that distinguish different rural areas when students discuss, negotiate and justify their choices?

When discussing careers, agency and place, I focus in particular on whether the students orient towards professions that require higher education, or towards low-skilled manual work. To explore young people's reflections on their careers in these respects is of particular interest in rural contexts. On the one hand, and as a result of the restructuring of jobs and businesses, and the closure of services, hospitals and schools, the need for highly trained staff with higher education qualifications has decreased in many rural areas. Yet on the other hand, and in relation to the wider national and global labour market, a university education is increasingly required to compete for the remaining attractive occupations. Consequently, what the highly educated student possesses has obvious implications for his/her position and attractiveness in both the local and wider labour market (Lundahl, 2011; Lundahl et al., 2014). This applies also to their positioning in society at large, as the social relations of production, skills, expertise, etc. constitute the foundation of class relations (Beach and Puaca, 2014; Nylund, 2012).

The analysis in this chapter concentrates on three schools (River School, Sea School and Coastal School). They are all located in small de/industrialised communities and they thus resemble each other in many ways. However, there were also some significant differences between them. One of them was related to how students reflected on their future careers, which is also the theme in focus in the present chapter.

After presentations of some key concepts, the analysis is reported in four sections. The first three sections discuss how students in three different rural schools/communities reflected on their careers. A fourth section summarises the analysis and discusses important factors in the process of shaping young people's ideas of future careers—their *reflexive practices* (cf. Farrugia, 2013).

Reflexive practices and local structural conditions

The concept of reflexivity is associated with late modernity and its elements of detraditionalisation, structural fragmentation and an ethic of individual free will and self-actualisation (Beck and Beck-Gernsheim, 2001; Beck et al., 1994). However, as argued by Farrugia (2013), individual reflexivity works in relation to local and wider structural conditions, and in the presented analysis I pay attention to factors such as gender, parental education and parents' position in the labour market, but also the characteristics of the places where the students live, especially the local material and social conditions (labour market and supply of education, proximity to educational opportunities, etc.). The impact of these factors has been examined by numerous empirical studies. From previous research we know that young people, to a great extent, tend to end up pursuing studies and working in occupations in accordance with patterns set by gender, class and the local environment in which they grew up (Beach and Puaca, 2014; Ball et al., 2000). This implies that social mobility is limited (e.g Furlong and Cartmel, 1997; Svensson, 2006; Biggart et al., 2015; Iannelli and Smyth, 2008). Drawing on these and other studies on social (im)mobility, we know that children who grow up with parents who are highly educated or who work as high-ranking officials in civil administration or business tend to orient towards continued academic studies, while children of lower officials, craft-oriented small entrepreneurs without education and manual workers, tend to orient towards vocational education and training. This is also reflected later in the labour market.Youths whose parents have working-class positions in the labour market and have weak educational backgrounds tend to end up with unskilled or low-skilled jobs in the service and care sectors to a greater extent than youths from more privileged backgrounds. Furthermore, the Swedish labour market is largely gender segregated (SCB, 2018), which means that gender also has a strong impact on how youths are positioned and tend to position themselves in the labour market. We may confidently assert that gender and class, as well as social and cultural socialisation patterns, have a great influence on the life paths of many young people (e.g. Svensson, 2006).

In addition, geographical places have distinct local structural factors and various types of infrastructures which can exert a profound influence. For example, different places have localised labour markets and distinct main industries, which in turn require different types of education and skills. In this way, many local places in themselves are gendered and classed. For example, in general the education level of people living in rural areas is lower than the education level of those living in urban places. Rural youth tend to choose vocational programmes to a greater degree than other young people, and they do not go on to higher education to the same extent that urban youths do (Statistics Sweden, 2016). Obviously, there are also infrastructural- and labour market-related differences between urban and rural areas which influence the sort of work people do. A high percentage of people living in rural areas have low- or modest-wage employment, such as unskilled work in the production and service sectors (Nylund, 2012). This, in turn, is due to the spatial pattern of the wider capitalist economy; to what Massey (1994) describes as the world economy's geometry of power relations, and what Harvey (2006) describes as a result of uneven geographical development. Neo-liberalism has contributed to profoundly restructuring the agricultural sector in rural spaces, but also other features of working and social life too, resulting often in the creation of difficult economic conditions in many rural areas through the closure of production and institutions and the development of new identities and articulations (Harvey, 2006, pp. 71-116).

When analysing the data, I looked for distinctive characteristics in the students' reflexive articulations, and read the data in relation to important structural factors such as gender and social class, but also in relation to the various local contexts—the local labour markets and their specific socio-spatial, material and infrastructural characteristics. It should be noted that what is in focus here is how the students *reflected* on and how they discussed their future (for example their plans for upper secondary education), not their actual and final decisions. This is important to bear in mind when considering the results. For example, it is unknown whether all students ended up studying/doing what they said they were intending to do—some might have changed their plans for various reasons.

The three rural locations

Like other small de/industrialised municipalities in rural Sweden, the municipalities where River School, Sea School and Coastal School were located have been exposed to national and global competitive economic forces over the last few decades. This has had various adverse effects, forcing the closure of whole industries and services (including educational institutions) and consequent depopulation, although this has happened to varying degrees. In this section, and as a complement to Table 1 in chapter one, the three municipalities are described in more detail, with the focus on the individual characteristics of the local labour market.

River School was located in a small town situated in a municipality within reach of four bigger cities (a range of some 100-150 kilometres). The local labour market was limited to the regional hospital, various smaller industries and a few power plants; a few middle-sized industries remained within commuting reach. The closure of a local military base and strong challenges to the industrial sector in recent decades had resulted in a contracting labour market as well as a decline in population since the 1980s (Statistics Sweden, 2016). A few workers commuted to the nearby cities on a weekly basis (usually craftsmen working on large building projects) and a few on a daily basis. The four nearby cities had varied labour markets, offering academic, white collar and various service and skilled industrial jobs. However, only a few people used this opportunity since commuting links were poor. Many of the parents of the students participating in the study represented the stable, small-town middle class; they worked in various service institutions and in health care, and there were also a few teachers and academics. A quarter of the students had migrant backgrounds, while most of the other students had parents who had lived in the region all of their lives.

Sea School was located in a village close to the sea, in a small municipality within approximately fifty kilometres of small and bigger cities in other municipalities; commuting to work in these towns was possible and quite usual. The municipality's administration centre was divided and situated in two different villages, one of them being the village where Sea School was located. Overall, the municipality was characterised by low educational levels among the population, and the local, heavily gendered labour market was, with one notable exception, mainly focused on small-scale factories and jobs in services and care. The biggest industry was forestry (a large hydroelectric plant had formerly been an important source of employment, but this had been lost with the plant's closure). The majority of the students' parents did low-skilled manual work. Few of the students' parents had an academic education, and where that was the case it was usually in the area of health care and teaching. About one-third of the students enrolled in the school class we visited had migrant backgrounds, while the rest usually had parents that had lived in the region all of their lives.

Coastal School was located in a central town in a geographically large community less than 100 kilometres from a big city. The local labour market was limited (mainly small-scale businesses and jobs in services and care), and strong challenges to the industrial sector in recent decades had resulted in the closure of many of the town's major businesses; however, some small enterprises, including handicraft and agricultural businesses, were still flourishing and contributed to a somewhat more varied and gender-integrated labour market. Furthermore, because the town was within commuting distance of a nearby city, people could work in the city and still live in the local community (or vice versa). The nearby city had a higher education institution, and a varied labour market offering academic, white collar and various service and skilled industrial jobs. The relative proximity to the city and good commuting links attracted small businesses to the local town, and provided residents with access to a greater and more varied labour market. As with River municipality, many of the parents of the students participating in the study essentially represented the stable, small-town middle classes, but there were also some who worked in jobs that traditionally represent working-class occupations. A general description is that most parents worked in various service and skilled industrial jobs, including both handicraft and agricultural businesses, but there were also teachers, academics, high-level civil servants in the municipalitiy's administration and a number of self-employed workers. A great majority of the students had non-immigrant backgrounds.

Something that also clearly distinguished the three municipalities was the varying range of educational opportunities, which meant that students were offered different possibilities for continuing education after secondary school. While River municipality had two lower secondary schools covering the region, there was only one lower secondary school in the Sea and Coastal regions, which meant that some students had long distances to travel to school. Furthermore, River town provided upper secondary education. As about two-thirds of the Swedish upper secondary education national programmes, among them the most popular ones, were offered there, most students could attend upper secondary education in River municipality. However, if they planned to choose one of the national programmes that were not on offer, or a special programme, it would be necessary to move away from home during the three years of upper secondary education.

In Sea and Coastal municipalities there were no upper secondary education institutions at all. In Coastal municipality, there used to be an upper secondary school, but it was closed down at the time of the study. No locally located upper secondary education institution meant that students living in Sea and Coastal municipalities needed to attend upper secondary education in another municipality, either by commuting or moving for the duration of their studies. For Coastal students, daily commuting was possible to three relatively nearby municipalities which offered upper secondary education, while the Sea students had fewer options. Also, the distance students had to travel to attend a higher education institution varied: Coastal students had a relatively short distance to travel, while their River and Sea counterparts faced quite long distances (see Table 1, chapter one). It should be mentioned that two of River's nearby cities had a higher education institution.

Students' reflections on careers and futures

In this section, the students' reflections on careers and futures are presented for each of the local places; the small, basically middle-class town that provided upper secondary education (River); the small working-class village where the educational level among the parents was low (Sea); and the former industrial small town with a social class mixture situated near to a big city (Coastal).

Preference for academic programmes in River School

In River School the students were clearly oriented towards academic programmes. In fact, all of the students in the River class planned to choose an academic programme since they thought that higher education was necessary for a *proper* profession. Among the girls, the most popular programme was social science. The most popular programme for the boys in the class was the natural science programme, which was considered to be excellent preparation for university studies. In the interviews it became clear that preference for the natural science programme was often linked to particular role models in the family. An illustrative example was Ron, who planned to choose the natural science programme and then apply for a university programme in the region. He also had the vision of one day working in a university. Ron's brother studied at the university in a large city in the region, and his mother also worked there, weekly commuting. When Ron reflected on what might have influenced him, he said:

Ron: Friends, I don't know, but my brother studies at the university and my mother works there, and I want to move there too [University city]. /..../ My brother is a political scientist, my mother is a pharmacologist. I would enjoy doing something like that. At least, I want to work at the university.

(River School, April 21)

It was obvious that the educational level of siblings and the position of parents within the labour market were influential factors when Ron and other students in River town reflected on their future; attending an academic programme with a view to then moving on to higher education was something that they strived for.

Staying or leaving is an issue that has often been highlighted in youth research and has been put forward as a central issue for rural youth in particular (e.g. Rosvall et al., 2018; Rönnlund, 2019; see also Bæck and Paulgaard, 2012). However, among the students in River School, the issue of *staying or leaving* was a rather vague presence. There was not much talk about where to live in the future, for example if one planned to move away or stay in the local community, or maybe—as in the case of Ron's mother—stay in River town but work elsewhere. One interpretation of this is that the leaving/staying issue was a project that lay quite a few years ahead for students in River town; there was a generous range of upper secondary programmes to choose between locally, so the question of moving/staying could wait until after upper secondary school. Another interpretation is that the students thought that moving into higher education and getting a *good* job was a much more important issue to them than their home residence:

Rolf: I don't want to have just any job. I want to have a job I like, as long as I can do what I want to do, I'm happy. Where I live is not that important. At least this is how I feel now.

(River School, April 20)

This distinct pattern—emphasising occupation as being much more important than place of residence—has been found to be a particular characteristic of middle-class youth; Ron and Rolf personified this in our study, but the trait has been found in other studies (Svensson, 2006; Beach and Puaca, 2014; Puaca, 2013). The scant attention paid to where to locate oneself might also have been an expression of the process of *letting go* of their hometown, and it may also be linked to how they perceived River in terms of job prospects. As articulated by Rolf:

> I think that there are not so many different jobs here. It can be hard to find just that job you feel you want to continue working with in your life. That is why I want to study at the university and go ahead and live in a big city. There are more opportunities there. A greater range of education and jobs, which means it's easier to focus on what one actually wants to do in life. (River School, April 20)

The quote indicates that Rolf felt his opportunities would be more limited if staying put in the local town, but extended if leaving—in a big city Rolf thought that he could focus on what he actually wanted to do in life.

As higher education and getting a *good* job was highly valued, there were rather intensive discussions about entry points to various programmes among the students in the River School class, suggesting a keen awareness that you need to have enough grades to get into a favourite programme and get on with your life. Most of the students worked hard and did not have to worry about getting into their first choice of upper secondary school. However, there were a few that felt aiming for a good career was already of pressing importance. The effects of peer pressure in this regard are crucial. As most of these students had parents with relatively long academic backgrounds, the general and dominating pattern was to plan for enrolling on academic programmes.

In their discussions it became obvious that two boys in the class were initially uncertain whether to choose a vocational or academic programme. Both went to a meeting where information on the vocational building and construction programme was provided, and shortly after this one of the boys openly said that he had decided to choose an academic programme. That strongly affected the other boy, who wanted a *companion* and did not want to be the only one opting for a vocational programme. Towards the end of the term this boy did everything he could to achieve good enough grades to enrol on the academic programme of his choice; he took extra classes and accepted one-to-one teaching when it was offered. Enrolling on a vocational programme was no longer considered an attractive option, although before the meeting about the building and construction programme he had said that he was quite sure he would choose it. Thus, it was not only parents and older siblings who exercised an influence—the choices made by peers also influenced upper secondary programme choices (cf. Petrin et al., 2014; Rosvall, 2015).

Preference for vocational programmes in Sea School

In Sea School, students reflected quite differently on their future careers compared to the River students. There was, for example, much less talk about higher education and getting an academic degree. About sixty per cent of the students planned to choose a vocational programme and had manual skilled professions in mind.[1] Furthermore, their preferences in terms of programmes and professions followed traditional gender patterns: building and construction and vehicle and transport were popular programmes among the boys, while health and social care was a popular programme among the girls (cf. Swedish National Agency for Education, 2016).

Sven was one of the students in the Sea school class who had decided to choose a vocational programme. He was an accomplished student, with an interest in motors and vehicles, and movies from the 1950s. In keeping with these interests, he planned to choose the vehicle and transport programme. He referred to his parents when talking about what programme to choose, and barely spoke about his friends. As with many other parents in the Sea region, Sven's parents worked in a small industry and in services, i.e. occupations that seldom require higher education. Sven's father worked in the service and tourism sector, and his mother at the local recycling centre performing service and administrative tasks; this was the workplace where Sven had one of his work experience placements (PRAO).[2] He had liked it there and saw working with transport at the recycling centre as desirable. By studying the vehicle and transport programme he hoped to get a job at the centre and go straight into production directly after having completed upper secondary school.

Sven was insistent about wanting to stay in Sea. His father lived away from Sea during weekdays, commuting to the workplace—this was something that did not attract Sven. He expressed admiration for the local community

1. When calculating frequencies, I draw on what they saw as likely choices, and categorised their answers accordingly, even if they expressed uncertainty (see also Rönnlund et al., 2018).
2. In Sweden, some schools offer short work experience periods (PRAO: *praktisk arbetslivsorientering*, literally 'practical working life orientation') at a workplace as part of education about the local and wider labour markets. However, this is not obligatory and some schools only provide classroom teaching about the subject.

(cf. Rönnlund, 2019), and wished to stay in the region and get a job in the transport sector. But he did not seem very optimistic about the feasibility of his ambition:

> Sven: I love this place, it's special [...] I'd really like to live here, I like the lake and I like x (a nearby small town), I want to stay in the region [...] But, I realise that I need to go where the jobs are, and they're in the big cities [...]. (Sea School, November 8)

Another of the students who preferred a vocational programme was Sofia. She planned to take the health and social care programme. Her father worked in local industrial production and her mother as a nursing assistant in the local health services, a care and service sector that Sofia also imagined herself working in. She was a succesful student, with high grades, yet she still claimed that studying was not her cup of tea. She wanted to get a job and start work straight after finishing school, but she was also open to the possibility of further studies later on:

> Sofia: Studying has never really been my thing. So, my plan is to choose the health and social care programme, then, later on, I might continue studying to become a nurse.
> (Sea School, December 15)

As there was no upper secondary education available in Sea, Sofia, like all of her classmates, had to leave to obtain an upper secondary education. However, she planned to return to Sea after upper secondary school, at least for *a while*:

> Sofia: I guess I'll move back here, and work as a nursing assistant; I can easily get a job at the local nursing home for elderly people. Earn some money, and then, after a while, I could take up my studies again.
> Interviewer: So, you plan to come back here after upper secondary?
> Sofia: Yes, for a while, to earn money [...]. But after becoming skilled as a nurse, I don't think I'll come back here.
> (Sea School, December 15)

Sofia emphasised her interest in health and medicine in both daily conversation and during the interview; at the beginning of the fieldwork she even talked about becoming a doctor. But, as shown in the above quote, she had a career as a nurse or nursing assistant in mind by the time of the interview. Thus, the cultural and social context may have influenced the occupation (doctor, nurse or nursing assistant) she identified with *within* the health and medicine sector when reflecting on her career, although of course it is not possible to know for sure. Moreover, her decisions seemed to be closely related to her ideas about where to live in the future: in Sea she saw herself as a nursing assistant, but as a nurse she saw herself living elsewhere. This might have been related to actual labour market conditions—there were not many jobs that required a nursing education in Sea, and those which did exist did not attract her. This might also be related to experienced constraints and local gender relations; Sofia saw herself as a nursing assistant within the social, cultural and geographical constraints of the local context, but as a nurse or doctor in other contexts. This underlines the importance of place in shaping processes of identity formation. A place is of course shaped by the people who live there, but the place itself also determines to a great extent its social relations and the degree of freedom the individual has (Massey, 1994).

This pattern of favouring vocational programmes and gender-typical choices among the students in Sea thus harmonised with their parents' position in the local labour market, and was consistent with local labour market conditions. Sea's labour market offered manual industrial jobs and service jobs that were more gender segregated than River's—a clear majority of the women worked in health or social care settings in the service sector, and the men in the few local industries. Thus, when reflecting on the future, the students' gender and their class backgrounds, their parents' position in the labour market in combination with the structural conditions of the particular local place where they lived were important influences—they chose programmes and reflected on their choices in accordance with these preconditions. In some cases, their educational and vocational choices can be understood as strategic selections, made in order to try to stay in their local place.

Furthermore, in comparison with the River students, Sea students placed much more emphasis on the issue of staying or leaving. Some Sea School students expressed a wish to stay in Sea after upper secondary school and emphasised the area's attractions and benefits. But they also expressed a concern that this was not possible and some kind of disclosure that they would probably have to move away from the limited labour market Sea had to offer. Their talk about moving indicated that they perceived their choices as limited and felt pressure to leave (cf. Corbett, 2013).

However, as a result of their class backgrounds the pupils seemed to experience this pressure differently. From the interviews it was obvious that their social background and the family's financial resources were important. There was only a limited selection of schools and programmes that were located within daily commuting distance. If someone wanted to study a special programme of some sort (such as an elite sports programme) he/she would have to move away from home during the upper secondary school period, and that was not an option available to everyone; living away from home results in significant additional costs, and all of the families did not have sufficient financial resources to pay for, for example, extra housing. That was the situation Sebastian was in. He wanted to go to a specialist programme in a city, but the financial situation of the family was a hindrance:

> *Sebastian:* Yes, I will probably move to x [nearby city]. My stepmother and me are searching for money so we can afford the rent.
> (Sea School, December 16)

From this and other examples I draw the conclusion that the Sea School students' reflections were framed and formed by their gender and social class background, and their families' economic situation and resources in terms of networks and personal contacts. Furthermore, these young people lived in a markedly classed and gendered locality with a specific economic class structure which probably also had an impact on how they thought about the future, for example whether they planned to invest in an academic programme or a vocational programme.

Interest in non-gender stereotyped choices in Coastal School

Coastal School stood out as a school where the students chose vocational and academic tracks to about the same extent. The general pattern was that they expressed an orientation towards programmes that were in line with their social background and the education and occupation of their parents. Students whose parents worked in high-skilled jobs discussed those kinds of jobs, while students with parents with low-skilled jobs talked about those kinds of jobs. As a whole, their reflections mirrored the varied and multifaceted labor market that Coastal town represented, and thus, the economic class structure that characterised the local place.

Coastal School was also distinctive because of the significant number of non-gender stereotyped career choices made by the students. One of the students who planned to make a *non-gender stereotyped* career choice was Kerstin. In the interview it became clear that she was fascinated by the occupation of lorry driver, although she also had other ideas of possible careers in mind:

> Kerstin: I want to take the vehicle and transport programme in x [small town more than 100 kilometres from Coastal]. But I am not sure; I would like to become an electrician also, in that case I will go to y [nearby city]. Or, a nail technician.
> (Coastal School, February 17)

Like many other students in Coastal School, Kerstin frequently referred to family members when she talked about the future (cf. Butler and Muir, 2016; Snee and Devine, 2014). Her brother was working as a lorry driver, and he used to take her with him on drives when she was younger. She also had male role models in her family doing manual work that she found interesting; this became obvious when she talked about where to do her PRAO. From Kerstin's reflections it became obvious that the careers of her family members provided her with ideas about doing her PRAO.

> Kerstin: My idea was first to do my PRAO at my brother's work place, he is a lorry driver, but he has got sick and won't be working for a while, so I got the idea to try to get a placement in a nail salon in [nearby city], but I'm afraid that they would not let me do nails, just watching, so right now, I'm thinking of going to do my PRAO at my uncle's work place who is a painter.
> (Coastal School, February 17)

The fact that some girls in Coastal School were interested in male-dominated programmes (a phenomenon which did not occur in the other places to the same extent) is interpreted as being related to the local labour market in the municipality, which, according to what the students said about their parents' jobs in the interviews, did not seem to be quite as gender-segregated as in the other places. In Sweden, like in many other countries, spatially differentiated trade and industry structures and the design of the public sector can differ between municipalities and regions, which creates different gender relationships in different places—this seemed to be the case here.

Another major distinction between Coastal and the other municipalities was its relatively close distance to a large city with a varied labour market offering academic, white collar and various service and advanced industrial jobs. Good commuting links to the city attracted small businesses to the local town, and gave people living there access to a greater and more varied labour market, something that was reflected in the variety of the parents' professions and occupations (which showed a variation that did not occur to the same extent in the other places). This diversity was also reflected in the female students' expressions of interest in traditional male occupations, which through being non-reciprocated by the boys, meant that study programmes leading towards traditional female occupations; such as health- and childcare were not sought-after. There was not one student who wanted to take the health and social care programme for instance, and only one who wanted to take the child and recreation programme. There seems to be a gender and class coding of education and employment. Male coded manual jobs and vocational programmes had a higher status than female coded ones.

The Coastal School students resembled the Sea School students concerning the extent to which they seemed to pay attention to the question of staying or leaving when talking about their future careers. They all needed to attend upper secondary education somewhere outside Coastal, and thus had to leave the town to study. Daily commuting was possible for some of them depending on what school and programme they decided on and got access to, but reflecting and deciding on which programme, school and location to go for, came in the same package. Thus, to these students, *where* to study and *where* to live in the future, e.g. whether to stay in the region and travel to school daily, or move away, was a great part of their reflections. For example, Kerstin wanted to study the vehicle and transport programme, a programme that was located in a small town at quite distance from Coastal, which made daily commuting difficult. She said she wanted to move there and live by herself during her upper secondary years. Thus, the vehicle and transport programme attracted her, but so did moving away from home. In fact she was rather firm about leaving Coastal as soon as possible, and this possibly influenced her will to study a programme that she couldn't get access to in the neighbourhood, and that made daily commuting almost impossible. Still, she was positive to coming back to Coastal town later on, for instance to have a family:

> Kerstin: [...] but when I get older or much older, I would like to come back here and live here or at least around here. I would be too stressed living in the city when I get old.
> (Coastal School, February 17)

Kerstin's reflections about what programme to study was thus linked to where she was going to live the nearest future. While some could not think of moving, she really wanted to get away from Coastal town for a time. But as the quote indicates, the question of where to live was also closely linked to age—as a young student/person she saw herself living in the city, whereas as an old person she saw her self living in Coastal town and its surroundings.

Discussion

There were some distinct carachteristics in how students reflected on their careers and futures between the three small, de/industrialised municipalities. Often, their ideas were apparently gendered and classed and in line with the material, structural and infrastructural characteristics of these largely rural regions—their reflections were culturally and socially situated (this will be further elaborated on in chapter six). For example, in Sea School, where education levels were low and the local labour market predominantly offered unskilled manual and service work, there was a stronger tendency to choose programmes oriented towards such occupations than in places with higher education levels (River School) and access to a more varied labour market (Coastal School). Likewise, there was an association between strongly gendered labour markets and gender-typical choices (Sea School). The students' knowledge and preferences about the world in terms of studies and careers was *positioned*, i.e. related to the spatially classed and gendered context they were placed in (cf. Massey, 1994).

Furthermore, the students' parents' work and position in the labour market was a component in their reflexive practices. When the students talked about their future studies and careers they often related their ideas to the education and occupations of their parents and siblings. For example, Ron envisioned studying and working at the university in the city, like his brother and mother, whilst Sven talked about working with transport at the local recycling centre like his mother. From this I draw the conclusion that close family members' occupations and positions in the labour market were influential on how the students visualised and understood what it meant to *work*. The parents' and older siblings' positioning within the labour market and their overall class background seemed to inform the young students' ideas about what people do for a living, and in that sense also *what people like me do*.

The students' reflections about study and career paths thus had notable contextual, classed and gendered dimensions. They were also, in various degrees, interwoven with ideas about real and imagined places, something that indicates that people's visions about the future are indeed shaped by specific local and regional conditions, but also by imagined and actual interactions with other regions and nations (cf. Massey, 1994). To reflect on one's future in spatial terms was most apparent for students living in rural localities without ready access to upper secondary school (Coastal School, Sea School). To them, reflecting on future studies inevitably meant thinking about location. To reflect on and negotiate study and career choices was thus a relational spatial practice in a double sense (cf. Massey, 1994): it was spatial in the sense that it was situated locally and thus marked by social class and the specific structure of local productive and social relations, but also spatial in terms of the fact that future studies and jobs were thought to be located somewhere. To reflect on *what* to do in the future for most of the students also included consideration of *where* this future will take place.

Thus, the variation between local rural places in how the students reflected on their future studies and careers, including the variation between students in the same locality, points at the influence of place, distance and individual positions in terms social class and gender in young people's thought about their futures. Still, this does not mean that the students lacked a reflexive attitude towards their future. Living in rural regions where industries and services have closed down, where there are limited opportunities for work and further studies, and where both young people and adults have a very limited selection of jobs to choose from, if any, can evoke a necessarily reflexive attitude to life (cf. Geldens and Bourke, 2008). This was also noticed in this data, demonstrating a variety of reflexing practices among the young people. But still, reflexivity always works in relation to local and wider conditions, such as access to jobs and education including distances to such features, and as the analysis shows, the conditions differed between the rural places. Together with gender and classed dispositions in terms of parental education and parents' position in the labour market, these factors have been proven to influence individuals' agency and life paths (cf. Beach and Puaca, 2014; Ball et al., 2000). What has been discussed in this chapter, is that they also tend to affect young individuals' reflexive practices, what they see as possible or desirable, i.e. how they reflect on their *imagined spatial futures* (cf. *spatial horizons* in Evans, 2016; see also Rönnlund, 2019). Thus, local conditions (which are to be understood in relation to wider socioeconomic structures) and individual dispositions both influence individuals' agency *and* affect the options individuals see as possible or desirable.

References

Bæck, U. D. and Paulgaard, G., (2012) (eds). *Rural futures? Finding one's place within changing labour markets*. Stamsund/Oslo: Orkana Akademisk.

Ball, S. J, Maguire M. and Macrae, S., (2000) *Choice, pathways and transitions post-16. New youth, new economies in the global city.* London: Routledge.

Beach, D. and Puaca, G., (2014) Changing higher education by converging policy-packages: Education choices and student identities, *European Journal of Higher Education*, 4(1): 67-79.

Beck, U. and Beck-Gernsheim, E., (2001) *Individualization. Institutionalized individualism and its social and political consequences.* London: Sage.

Beck, U., Giddens, A. and Lash, S., (1994) *Reflexive modernisation: Politics, tradition and aesthetics in the new modern order*. Cambridge: Polity Press.

Biggart, A., Järvinen, T. and Parreira do Amaral. M., (2015) Institutional frameworks and structural factors relating to educational access across Europe, *European Education*, 47(1): 26-45.

Butler, R. and Muir, K., (2017) Young People's education biographies. Family relationships, social capital and belonging, *Journal of Youth Studies*, 20(3): 316-331

Corbett, M., (2013) I'm going to make sure I'm ready before I leave: the complexity of educational and mobility decision-making in a Canadian coastal community, *Journal of Rural Studies*, 32: 275-282.

Evans, C., (2016) Moving away or ataying local. The role of locality in young people's 'spatial horizons' and career aspirations, *Journal of Youth Studies*, 19(4): 501-516.

Farrugia, D., (2013) Young people and structural inequality. Beyond the middle ground, *Journal of Youth Studies*, 16(5): 679-693.

Furlong, A. and Cartmel, F., (1997) Risk and uncertainty in the youth transition, *Young* 5(1): 3-20.

Geldens, P. M. and Bourke, L., (2008) Identity, uncertainty and responsibility: Privileging place in a risk society, *Children's Geographies*, 6(3): 281-294.

Harvey, D., (2006) *Spaces of global capitalism: Towards a theory of uneven geographical development.* London: Verso

Iannelli, C. and Smyth, E., (2008) Mapping gender and social background differences in education and youth transitions across Europe, *Journal of Youth Studies*, 11(2): 213-232.

Lawson, V., Jarosz, L. and Bonds, A., (2010) Articulations of place, poverty and race: Dumping grounds and unseen grounds in the rural American Northwest, *Annals of the Association of American Geographers*, 100(3): 655-677.

Lundahl, L., (2011) Paving the way to the Future? Education and young Europeans' paths to work and independence, European *Educational Research Journal,* 10 (2): 168-179.

Lundahl, L., Lidström, L., Lindblad, M., Lovén, A., Mårald, G. and Svedberg, G., (2014) No particular way to go. Careers of young adults lacking upper secondary qualifications, *Journal of Education and Work,* 30(1): 39-52.

Massey, D., (1994) *Space, place and gender.* Cambridge: Polity press.

Nylund, M., (2012) The relevance of class in education policy and research. The case of Sweden's vocational education. *Education Inquiry,* 3(4): 591-613.

Petrin, R. A., Schafft, K. A. and Meece, J. L., (2014) Educational sorting and residential aspirations among rural high school students: What are the contributions of schools and educators to rural brain drain? *American Educational Research Journal,* 51(2): 294-326.

Puaca, G., (2013) *Educational choices of the future: a sociological inquiry into micro-politics in education.* Diss. Gothenburg: University of Gothenburg.

Rönnlund, M., (2019) 'I love this place, but I won't stay'. Identification with place and imagined spatial futures amongst youth living in rural areas in Sweden, Young. 28 (2),. https://journals.sagepub.com/doi/pdf/10.1177/1103308818823818

Rönnlund, M., Rosvall, P.-Å. and Johansson, M., (2018) Vocational or academic track? Study and career plans among Swedish students living in rural areas, *Journal of Youth Studies,* 21(3): 360-375.

Rosvall, P.-Å., (2015) 'Lad' research, the reproduction of stereotypes? Ethnographic dilemmas when researching boys from working-class backgrounds, *Ethnography and Education,* 10: 215-229.

Rosvall, P.-Å., Rönnlund, M. and Johansson, M., (2018) Young people's career choices in Swedish rural contexts: Schools' social codes, migration and resources, *Journal of Rural Studies,* 60: 43-51.

Snee, H. and Devine, F., (2014) Taking the next step. Class, resources and educational choice across the generation, *Journal of Youth Studies,* 17(8): 998-1013.

Statistics Sweden., (2016) Kommunfaktablad 2016 [Basic facts about the municipality]. Retrieved from http://www.scb.se/

Statistics Sweden., (2018) Gender statistics. https://www.scb.se/en/finding-statistics/statistics-by-subject-area/living-conditions/gender-statistics/gender-statistics/. Statistics Sweden.

Svensson, L., (2006) *Vinna och försvinna? Drivkrafter bakom ungdomars utflyttning från mindre orter.* [To win or disappear? Driving forces behind young people's migration from small places] Diss. Linköping Studies in Arts and Science No 359. Linköpings universitet.

Swedish National Agency for Education., (2016) *Uppföljning av gymnasieskolan. Regeringsuppdrag—uppföljning och analys av gymnasieskolan.* Stockholm: Skolverket [National Agency for Education]. Follow-up of Upper Secondary School.

Chapter 5

Places and schools in times of demographic change

Monica Johansson

Introduction

The demographic processes connected to rural (and urban) areas vary over time and place, with populations either being pushed out of the rural areas or drawn into them, often in association with changing relations of economic production. These are global phenomena (Balfour, Mitchell and Moletsane, 2008) that raise questions of direct relevance to our *Rural youth* project. Based on the data my colleagues and I collected, this chapter addresses a question posed by Massey connected to these issues (1994, p. 147): "What is it that determines mobility and that influences the sense we have of space and place?" More specifically, it considers responses of places and schools in relation to migration, and how these changes can be understood in connection to participation and integration of groups and individuals in the researched rural places. Particular concerns are responses of students and teachers related to demographic processes in the local communities and schools and demographic change. However, as we could not follow developments in the places and schools over a long period it is important to stress that the depth and durability of the observed recent intensive changes will only become apparent in the future.

A feature of the places included in our research, and frequently of education in rural places in other countries (Hargreaves, Kvalsund, and Galton, 2009; Sørensen and Pless, 2017), is that the residents often have a cohesive life story connected to the place that extends at least two generations. Even when younger generations express plans to move in the future (as some of our participants did, see chapter four) there is usually a desire to return at some point, either regularly (often seasonally) or permanently.

In the researched schools, many students and teachers have a long connection to the place and have expressed relationships with one another, the place and its history, as described also elsewhere (e.g. Holm, 2008; Svensson, 2010). However, there are also inhabitants who have moved into the place for diverse reasons and at varying times, largely from other parts of Sweden, north-western Europe, and (most recently) Syria and neighbouring countries. In this chapter the focus is on these three groups of migrants.

There are three main reasons for the migration from other parts of Sweden (and in some cases the neighbouring country Norway). Some people have returned to the place where they grew up, to be closer to family and relatives. They have often also been given work opportunities in the place (or can commute to places nearby). Some have been attracted by cheap farms and/or attractively situated houses, by lakes for example. Finally, our data show that in some cases personal life circumstances have contributed to the move. These are primarily related to changes in social relations, such as marriage, divorce, or death in the family and (specifically for some of the students) placement in the care of Social Services.

Migrants from other north-west European countries, for example the Netherlands and the Baltic countries, are often entrepreneurs or otherwise engaged in various occupations connected (for instance) to the environmental and outdoor recreational sectors. Issues frequently mentioned during the interviews as contributing to this migration include beautiful natural environments, the scope for outdoor activities, vast sparsely populated areas and the associated physical and individual spaces.

The time in which the research group carried out the field studies coincided with several global changes, including upheavals that had contributed to a large increase in numbers of refugees coming to Sweden from Syria (Swedish Migration Agency, 2015; 2017). The six places and associated schools covered in the field studies received varying numbers of refugees, providing opportunities to examine how new groups of international migrants (see also Hedberg and Haandrikman, 2014) have mixed and interacted with the local communities and schools. Thus, the influx enabled us to address very rapid and unpredicted contemporaneous demographic change and how schools and people in them were able to respond to this and were supported politically and by the local community in this response.

To illustrate the scale of these changes, 163,000 asylum seekers were received in 2015 (134,000 of them during the second half of the year), but in 2016 the number of refugees decreased by eighty-two per cent (Swedish Migration Agency, 2015; 2017). The big cities received the largest numbers of migrants in absolute terms, but the smaller communities, including some in quite sparsely populated areas, received higher numbers relative to their populations (Swedish Schools Inspectorate, 2016; 2015). During this process, the schools shouldered a lot of responsibility for the education and welfare of newly arrived children and youths (Nilsson and Bunar, 2016), as clearly highlighted in our observations.

The chosen theoretical framework of the project treats place as being constantly in a process of construction and reshaping on and through social relations with linkages, tensions, solidarities, dependences and interdependences between groups that shift with time (Massey, 1994). We have used it together with theories of social class, which we defined, following Harvey (1996), broadly in terms of human situatedness and positionality (see chapter one). This is a definition that links well with Massey's spatial perspective and facilitates analysis of rural societies as constituted by people with diverse demographic profiles living within various social, cultural and economic relationships (Argent, 2016). We have also, in this chapter (in a more experimental way) tried to applied concepts formulated by Bourdieu (1987). We ask how place, space and time together with various forms of capital influence individuals and groups both position themselves and are positioned by others in different social fields. In this, we have recognised that position, field (settings of agents and their interactions) and habitus (physical embodiment of capital) influence how and where people live their lives to generate a feeling of being in the *right place* or not (Callewaert, 1996; Rönnlund and Tollefsen, 2016). Later in the chapter, in the discussion section, I apply these concepts to analyse how different forms of capital have interactively helped to maintain or change power structures.

Results

The empirical results are presented in three parts of this section. The first, entitled "New locals' voices about their respective places and schools", concerns some of the new locals' views of the places and schools and how they compare the new place and school in relation to with their earlier experiences. The second section, entitled "The importance of blending in and knowing one's place", highlights challenges for newcomers in the places and schools. The third, entitled "The places and schools in times of change", concerns changes in the places and schools, and how both old and new locals talk about possible changes. The results section concludes with an analysis of the empirical material based on Bourdieu's concepts of capital.

New locals' voices about their respective places and schools

The students in the researched areas were dependent on adults' decisions and had little influence over choices of places to live and schools to attend. Following many family events, for example divorce, if one or both parents move(s) children often have to go with them, whether they want to or not, as there are simply no other options for most families. Some of the newcomers in the participating schools had moved under such conditions, but different circumstances had dictated the movement to the area for most of them (including those specifically addressed here) even more profoundly. This should be noted, because earlier and potentially radically different experiences of childhood and life conditions are likely influence recently arrived students' perceptions of a place and school.

Being a newcomer

A general pattern from our observations and interviews, which has been frequently found also in other rural studies (Rye, 2006), is that the newcomers described the places in positive terms, highlighting their closeness to nature, calmness, comfort and safety (chapter two). However, the perceived calm is associated with paucity of cultural possibilities, remoteness and inadequate public transport, such as bus services (Sørensen and Pless, 2017). Some students and adults also described difficulties in establishing contacts with people who have lived in the places for a long time and joining the communities in the researched places and schools.

For Shahid and Sam, who had both moved (for reasons dictated by Social Service) from Stockholm (the capital of Sweden), experiences of their new rural environment had been predominantly positive. Independently of each other they talked in an almost romantic way about the calmness of the place, with low crime rates and no drugs, making it easier to grow up there than in the big cities. As Shahid said, 'There are no criminals'. He also used the word *farmland* when talking about the place, but stressed that he thought, 'This is good'. When Sam talked of his experiences, he stressed that he liked 'The silence, calm and space', which are mainly to do with nature and compared it favourably to his experiences of Stockholm. However, Sebastian (who also moved to the area from a larger city for reasons dictated by Social Services) described the opposite; he saw few advantages of living in the countryside and wanted to return to a bigger city as soon as possible. The lack of public transport, friends and things to do were his main criticisms.

New students' expressed perceptions of the schools were also generally positive, with some exceptions, especially those of students who had experiences of schools in the territorially stigmatised suburbs of major cities in Sweden and also sometimes more authoritarian school systems in other countries. Our participants also included some students who had hardly attended school at all, mainly due to poverty, war and being on the move for several years. Despite the obvious hardships associated with fleeing; including uncertain life situations and a new language; several of them perceived and described their new rural schools as better than what they had previously experienced. Their main comment was that the classes and relationships between teachers and students were more relaxed, easy-going and positive than in their previous experiences of education. As Shahid said:

> It's a good school, at least compared to other schools I've been to. The teachers didn´t care there, but here they do.
>
> (Sea School, November 6)

As for negative views, some students who had recently arrived as refugees complained that there was less structure and order in lessons than in schools they had previously attended. This seemed to restrict their chances to participate in the daily schoolwork, for reasons that were only partially due to being new and having to cope with a new language. It also illustrates how students' previous knowledge and personal experiences influenced perceptions of the new rural schools (see also Stenbacka, 2012). Further, the experiences seemed connected to a strong wish to be part of the school community, succeed in schoolwork and understand what was happening and this wish was also connected to challenges and difficulties that are highlighted in the second section.

The importance of blending in and knowing one's place

Some of the school staff also had experiences of moving into the areas and expressed difficulties in becoming part of the community. One teacher who had worked for a long time in one of the schools talked about being seen as a highly educated person and being met with respectful distance when she moved to the place and began working as a teacher. However, responses had changed over time, and she said she was no longer treated with such unwanted deference.

Another teacher who also had moved into the area said that one had to be cautious and avoid being a *fintaleter* (a dialectical Swedish expression meaning acting or thinking that you are special or more important than anyone else). Instead, one should follow *jantelagen* (literally 'Jante's law', a more broadly understood expression in Nordic contents meaning conforming and not displaying undue personal ambition or boastfulness). In an interview she expressed this sentiment (which also applied to the students) as follows:

Interviewer: I was talking to the teacher responsible for the three students in the Upper Secondary School who stay at the accommodation for refugees …

Staff: Yes, they live at the accommodation for refugees by the main road and have not been given residents' permits yet, they're waiting for them. Then we've had students who've been well integrated and weren't refugees. They've come for other reasons but from different parts of the world and they've been quite well integrated. In some way this is connected to ranking and I think that's part of the countryside too. It's not that easy to get used to being new and that. I wasn't brought up here either, but I've lived here so long I suppose it feels like I was. But if I force myself to think about it I think that for many years, probably ten, in the beginning I said I didn't feel like I belonged. I was a bit suspicious, the locals here is not supposed to be *fintaleter*. Do you understand that expression?... It's close to *jantelagen* and extremely strong. One is not supposed to be *fintaleter* and not really supposed to be too well educated either/

(Forest School, March 27)

Some students at Forest School expressed similar experiences. They perceived that new people in the place and school should *not be cocky*. They said that new people cannot just join the *cool kids*; new students have to adapt and wait to be accepted. Therefore, the experiences of both teachers and students highlighted the importance of *knowing your place* as a newcomer, which is not an easy platform to participate in a new environment. The next part more deeply explores the importance of families' historical connections to place for participation.

The power of a family history connected to place

As described above, a feeling that *everybody knows everybody*, permeating a place (see also chapter two) has profound implications for arrivals. Family, kinship and historical connections (or lack thereof) have strong apparent importance and seem to strongly affect the situations of newcomers and their chances to participate in the places and schools. One Sea School student, Stina, who was from a family with a long history in the area, described both positive and negative aspects, as follows:

The advantage is that ... you know who almost everybody is when you start secondary school in year seven, you know who the people are. But they live here, and you can't avoid them at all. And you know everybody, or who they are, and that might be nice. The disadvantage may be that the teachers know who you are outside of school too. That's the thing that's not so good. (Sea School, November 10)

The *everybody* here includes both close family members and more broadly friends and relatives, past and present. Another student, Silva, also described what it was like to grow up in a place where everybody knows whose child and grandchild you are, in a similar fashion to Stina's remarks:

My dad's really from Småland [an area in southern Sweden] but they moved here during his childhood, so he's always found his way back here and everybody knows who my dad is. So it's the same for me, I can go somewhere and then they ask me my name and that doesn't give anything away because I have my mum's surname. Then I say I'm X's daughter and everybody knows who I am and who he is. It's the same for me as for Stina! (Sea School, November 10)

The importance of kinship highlighted by Silva and Stina has been noted in previous research (Holm, 2008). Of course, for some of the students, including those who came as refugees, family history and kinship have little or no connection to their new places and lack such local potency (positive or negative).

New challenges faced by refugees

Unprecedented changes occurred when a relatively large number of refugees came, rapidly and without prior notice, to the focal places and schools. This posed certain challenges, as accommodation and schooling had to be arranged with little warning, often without knowing the exact numbers of new students before they arrived. The municipal authorities were also already short of both money and qualified staff, which exacerbated the problems.

There were both positive and negative interpretations and experiences of the resulting situation, in line with previous findings (Stenbacka, 2012). The staff at the school and some of the students spoke of risks of conflicts between different social groups, fuelled by (and potentially exacerbating) xenophobia and racism. However, there was little indication that such concern arose from first-hand experience and knowledge. It may have been fuelled by racist or sensationalist media coverage, or the influence of right-wing extremist channels and attitudes. On the other hand, there was also talk of advantages, such as increases in the population and job opportunities (even if these were few and temporary), as well as growth and development of the schools through the introduction of students who wanted to learn and were strongly motivated to study. As discussed below, both conflicts and solidarity were apparent, but also often silences about the situation in the local communities and schools.

Conflicts and solidarity

Important deficiencies included a lack of teachers with sufficient language skills to teach the new students, and shortages of space for all the new students so that previously quiet areas and corridors became crowded with students. In some schools, the newly arrived students were placed in *preparation classes* that focused on teaching Swedish and were hosted (for example) in spaces that students had previously used during breaks. Thus, before, between and after lessons all the other students spent most of their time in the corridors.

Both the teachers and students tried to understand and respond sympathetically to problems associated with the newcomers, and help efforts to find solutions to them. *Inter alia*, the situation was often discussed in meetings of Sea School's Student Council, as illustrated by the following field notebook excerpt:

> It is very lively in the corridor and the students suggested raising that question in their own classes again. A quiet and calm room where the students can relax is wanted [such a room was previously available, but the preparation class now have their lessons there] … The table tennis rackets are missing and there is still too much noise in the corridors. … One student, from grade 9, says that the students in the preparation class are not familiar with the school rules, because they still don't know the Swedish language. He can understand that they might need their own rackets. (Sea School, November 12 and December 8)

The Student Council members tried to find solutions to deal with the lack of space in the school. The atmosphere and discussions were sometimes critical, but often showed an understanding of what it might be like to arrive as a refugee and many of the students, teachers and local residents expressed strong solidarity with the newcomers and wanted to help them to participate in the schools' activities. The locals also tried to handle the situation, sometimes pointing to benefits for the municipality and searching for ways to address difficult aspects in both the municipalities and schools. A staff member in one of the schools spoke of the influx of refugees creating *explosive* changes for the place and school, particularly emphasising how little time the school and staff had to handle the organisational challenges.

> *Staff:* Three buses (with refugees) arrived this weekend. We have no idea how many children there are, and we know nothing more than the information the local administration has published. We got it first, then they published it on the website.
> *Interviewer:* And how are you handling the situation?
> *Staff:* We're waiting for information. But at the same time of course we must try to start recruiting teachers who can take care of them, and then the buildings of course. Not even the big councils have enough staff to handle this. The situation right now is a challenge for the school, indeed for the whole of Sweden.
> (Inland School, October 14)

The situation was described as critical not just in the local context but also in bigger municipalities across the whole country. However, the activities in our researched areas often focused on solving the immediate practical problems when time was very short. People who came to the areas needed places to sleep and eat, and in the schools there were urgent needs for space and teachers. Moreover, some of the newcomers were unaccompanied refugee children who had often experienced dramatic escapes from war-torn areas. In all six municipalities, special accommodation was arranged for these young refugees, staffed by local residents who often liaised with the schools on their behalf. The arrangements connected to the newcomers also contributed to the local labour market in some cases. For example, grocery shops were able to stay open longer. From the perspective of some of the locals, the newcomers also made the small places busier, not as silent and empty as previously. As one remarked, 'There's a lot more people in the village now'.

Many of the activities connected to solidarity focused both on groups and individual newcomers. Some of the local residents opened their homes and provided accommodation for the young newcomers. In the local area, churches and sport clubs arranged activities, and in many of the places the football clubs had particularly important roles in these activities. Some of the young male newcomers played and quickly became successful in the local football teams. Moreover, the importance of sport, especially football, was evident in many of the schools both during and between lessons. For some of the students, sport provided a way to participate in both the school and local place, or even plans for their future life. The local societies and schools also responded positively, appreciating the new members' initiative and efforts, and wanting them to succeed and progress. In addition, the importance of football was specifically stressed for a particular upper secondary program during an information event for year 9 students of Sea School, held in the upper secondary school in a nearby municipality:

> I follow the group who want to take a specific programme connected to football. From the class at Sea School there are four boys, three who have grown up in the area and one who recently arrived in Sweden. A teacher from the *football program* talks with the students (small talk) and asks who are from Sea School, and if they knew XX [a successful player from the surrounding area]. All of the students from Sea say that they knew him and the teacher jokes that the whole group can take the rest of the day off if they beat Sea School's team.   (Sea School, November 27)

Here the newly arrived student had a chance to participate in a group, in something that was a highly valued part of the daily life in the area. Being a successful part of a team gave him some chances to participate that he (and the team) could use in the future.

Silence

During the fieldwork there were some silences that surprised us as researchers (see also chapter three). Some important aspects, and even the immigrants' presence, provoked at most brief comments during our observation periods, as noted in the reflection below from the observations:

> The newly arrived immigrants are highly visible when you walk in the streets and in the large open areas in the school, where students of Swedish origin rarely spend time or just pass through to get to the canteen. However, there is more or less silence about them in classes,

Places and schools in times of demographic change   93

conversations between classes and in interviews if I do not specifically ask questions about their presence and associated issues. I have now conducted more than half of the interviews and it is interesting that very few of the students, teachers or head teachers spontaneously talk about the recent influx of immigrants. The only spontaneous comments about these matters I have heard were made (independently) by two interviewed boys with Swedish background, and concerned conflicts with immigrants that they had heard about.   (River School, April 27)

The re-organisation of space to accommodate the new arrivals was highly visible but rarely openly spoken about in River school. It was almost as if the immigrants were not there, although they obviously were. This silence was also noted in other researched schools when there were discussions about lack of space and the reasons for it. For example, a teacher in Sea School said, 'Yes, you know what I mean' (Sea School, December 1), when implicitly acknowledging that shortages were due to a large group of new students.

The places and schools in times of change

This final result section focuses more specifically on the demographic changes, looking both back and forward in time, in relation to the places and schools. First, I present voices of those who had lived a long time in the area, and their perceptions of the places, schools and how they had changed. Next, I describe and analyse how the new inhabitants may have contributed to the changes, and their possibilities to participate. Finally, I address issues related to handling changes in both short and long (lifetime) perspectives for both individuals and different groups. As previously stressed, our research covered very limited periods of time, and our findings do not indicate the durability of noted changes or their subsequent consequences, except insofar that they may provide indications of general patterns.

Reduction in numbers of inhabitants

When staff in the schools who had a long historical connection to the place and the school described and talked of changes, they mainly spoke of migration from the place and the consequent deterioration for the remaining inhabitants. This was particularly obvious in sparsely populated areas and is also a pattern from other Swedish research (see e.g. Hedlund et al., 2017; Hedberg and Haandrikman, 2014). The difficulties described contributed to a general decline in living conditions and exacerbated problems such as lack of work, inadequate public transport and difficulties in day-to-day running of schools when students, teachers and resources were all steadily decreasing. These are deleterious effects of long-term migration *from* the places, particularly in sparsely populated areas, and even though the recent influx of refugees had provided at least temporary respite from some of this decline, despite hopes of future improvement no one really seemed to believe that there might be long-term changes for the better. They suggested instead that by far the best option for young people was to move somewhere else. This applied generally, although there were some differences between both individuals and places. Interviewed adults in Inland School emphasised that the students' choices were limited, and staying in the area was risky due to the limited work opportunities. They painted a rather unpromising picture of the future:

> The students must move away from here or commute. Also, relatively few young people come back here, and that is, of course, not surprising considering the poor job opportunities we have here. The job prospects here are gloomy. (Inland, November 2)

Similarly, the study and career counsellor in Inland School said that she usually tells students who intend to stay in the local town that 'It will be tough'. However, heeding advice to move is easier for youths whose families have sufficient material resources to assist them, as also revealed during the field studies at River School:

> At lunch, some other teachers join us and ask about the study. A discussion commences about the place and its future. One teacher says that although it has its own upper secondary school, he does not want his own children to continue their studies here. He thinks his children should move as soon as possible. I ask if it is not expensive to accommodate your children when they study somewhere else. Pointing to the other teachers at the table, he answers that they are academics and although their wages are not as high as in urban areas they are still high in relation to their expenses. 'We bought our house ten to twenty years

ago for almost nothing and pay almost no interest. We can afford to buy a small apartment for our children during their studies'.

(River School, January 26)

The advice and statements above clearly suggest that teachers saw moving away as the logical option for the youths, due to the paucity of local work and education possibilities. Such moving away is an ongoing process that decreases numbers of inhabitants in rural areas (Argent, 2016). Moreover, the teachers also problematised the need and possibilities to move in financial terms, noting that some families cannot send their children to upper secondary school in another place, because they cannot afford the additional accommodation costs (see also chapter four). As noted by Fjellman, Yang Hansen and Beach (2018), they are stuck with what is on offer locally within the region, and almost completely lack the sorts of options promised by neoliberal idealists before market-oriented reforms in the education sector. In this respect, at least, market solutions seem to be poor arbiters of educational justice and inclusion.

Migration into the places and effects on the schools

The schools have had to cater for the increase in total numbers of students arising from the influx of refugees, and arrange education for the newly arrived students quickly, almost from scratch, without additional resources. This has been challenging for the schools and affected many parts of their operations. As already mentioned, the increases in numbers of students led to shortages of space in some schools, both in classrooms and other areas such as recreational areas and corridors. This was discussed by both teachers and students, as mentioned above and reported in chapter three. The observed (re-)organisation of educational activities spanned a spectrum from rapidly integrating the new arrivals in existing classes for all lessons to educating the newly arrived students in a separate group for a substantial time. Intermediate arrangements included (as a common example) keeping all the students together for practical aesthetics subjects, but separating the new students for Swedish lessons. All arrangements involved obvious changes, but the more integrative arrangements resulted in the most extensive changes in everyday school life:

> The immigrant students are integrated as soon as possible into regular classes and today two boys from north-east Africa have been to the Aesthetic class and now Crafts. I tried to talk to them during Aesthetics,

but they do not speak Swedish or English. Now during crafts, they are carving butter knives while the other boys make Sami knives with reindeer horn. The boys with an African background have placed themselves apart from the other students. (River School, April 28)

The changes engendered by the arrival of large groups of new students can place strains on teachers and students and the organisational responses have also had effects on the schools. However, generally positive views about new arrivals' effects on the schools and education they provided were expressed, indicating not only tolerance and acceptance but also an experience of value.

Some teachers noted that the newly arrived students were strongly motivated to learn and thus had a positive overall influence on the school. In the schools, there were also occasional examples of students, teachers and parents using their influence to protect and help the newly arrived students. They did this in a strong, committed and united way, using various strategies (e.g. collecting money, contacting newspapers and communicating with the Swedish Migration Agency) to increase the newly arrived students' chances to stay in the school and area. These activities and engagement also continued, as noted in one school, after one of the students (and the student's whole family) had been deported, and contact with both the student and the family has been maintained. In addition to the strong social relations, this shows that some changes in the places and schools can be linked to the schools' democratic tasks, and specifically to fostering solidarity among people, which is an explicit aim of the national curriculum (Lgr 11, 2018).

Although migration *from* the place emerged as the main driver of changes in the places, some of the migration into them seems to have prompted increases (or at least reduced declines) in levels of some services, such as availability of grocery stores, childcare and health centres. Further, some of the migration has been based on tourism, which has continued to provide local job opportunities, for example, jobs related to winter sports. The rapid influx of international refugees has also boosted work opportunities, for example in schools and social services. Moreover, it has led to increases in the places' liveliness as more people were moving around on the streets and marketplaces according to some participants and field observations.

Different ways to handle changes

The inhabitants expressed strategies for handling changes both currently and later in their lives that ranged from moving away as soon as possible to staying. In both cases (and intermediate strategies), what was regarded as desirable and possible depended on the individual's life circumstances and available resources, particularly opportunities for education and work. They were clearly connected to the material and cultural conditions, and liable to change over time. The predominant plan for youths in most of the places was to move, particularly in the sparsely populated areas and smaller industrial communities. That does not mean that all youths wanted to move (see chapter four), but they saw few possibilities for staying given the limited local opportunities for education and later employment, as expressed by one of the staff:

> And what is typical for the young people here is that most of them don't return once they've left after finishing upper secondary school. There's a clear line after grade 9 when they disappear never to come back. (…) maybe youths have always said, 'Oh my God I'm not coming back here' but here it is a reality because one both thinks and understands that it isn't even possible. In addition, this is not a nice thing to say … but if you look at the ones who stay, they are not the ones with high grades.
> (Forest School, March 27)

The impression here is that moving from this declining area following the collapse of the local timber and pulp industries is the most obvious option for any youths who can move, and that those who do stay are those with the lowest resources, weakest grades and hence fewest choices (Stockdale, 2004). However, our data also include records of some youths explicitly expressing desires to stay in the places, including (interestingly) some young people who had newly moved into them. Rosvall (2017) also noted such desires, with gender differences, in plans expressed for the future by five students with an immigrant background at River school. The girls planned to move to a bigger town for education and work, but the boys thought that as immigrants they may experience less stigma in the rural area and wanted to stay. For some people who had fled war zones the perceived tranquillity and safety of the rural areas were understandably attractive. Some of the newly arrived students also expressed a wish to stay and participate in the development of Sweden. For example, one of the students (Suresh) said in response to a question about how he thought about the future:

> Yes, we can [influence] the future! We can do it because when we're at University and then five years later we work for Sweden. For example, we can work maybe in health and social care, and maybe as car mechanics. We can help Sweden. (Sea School, November 6)

Envisaging a future where he, as a young newly arrived person in a rural area, can 'help Sweden', Suresh seemed to see himself, and other young immigrants, as youths who would like to use education as a means to stay in the country and the area, by developing personal skills, knowledge and hence a capacity to participate in and contribute to society in diverse and genuinely useful ways. This vision is consistent with conclusions reached by the Swedish parliamentary Countryside Committee (SOU: 2017), that asylum seekers and new arrivals are highly important for future rural development. Our data also indicate that the communities and schools responded positively to, and tried to handle the changes in circumstances caused by their arrivals quickly and effectively to promote these possibilities. They often tried to provide support by showing strong empathy toward, and care and tolerance for, the new students. Moreover, the students responded by showing gratitude and expressing a desire to accept what was on offer and engage with the school and community to develop personally and give something back to their new society.

Thus, we noticed silence and some conflicts in relation to the big groups of refugees. However, a main conclusion from our study is that the new arrivals have been broadly welcomed and supported by the local rural communities and their members. Another is that they are happy to be in the communities and want to give something back for the generosity they have received. In sum, they are recognised as welcome additional potential future resources, as both individuals and groups, for the places, and have strong commitment to reciprocate. This is a very different impression from the scaremongering stories about migration and migrants, and the racially hostile messages of extreme (and increasingly mainstream) political parties and their policies. In this respect, educational relations seem to be situated in the centre of a positive dialectic in the observed social processes of power and participation related to demographic change.

Discussion

In the chapter, I have considered factors that affect a sense of belonging, participation, inclusion and integration into local communities. Factors that clearly emerged as important in these respects are kinship and mutual history.

However, our data show that successful participation in local traditions and activities can also be related to forms of capital that help to create possible social bonds and bridges. Sports for example have been shown to work in these ways and our data also reveal the importance of social learning in relation to behavioural norms for fitting in, such as refraining from showing-off or acting as if one is *special*.

Economic capital is obviously important in relation to migration flows in and out of an area. The early capitalist processes of primitive accumulation has become so socially engrained as to have become hegemonic in ways that have led to the forced movement of the proletariat to areas where it is possible (or easier) to earn a living being normalised or naturalised. It represents a form of primary economic mobility and this is the primary form of *free mobility* into and out of rural areas. However, access to sufficient economic capital also allows parents to send their children away to study in other areas or bigger towns if they want, or feel a need to do so, and they may not return. Thus, substantial proportions of economic capital have to leave the areas because of the basic lack of sufficient investment in them by the State to uphold basic services. It is a kind of response to change that is difficult to counter for the areas' inhabitants that is also tied to national politics, of course, and the recent migrant infusion can be considered here. This new migration has triggered increases in parts of the labour market connected to social services and other provisions in the areas, which respondents regarded favourably. But these are temporary, publicly financed service category jobs and we cannot predict the duration or long-term consequences of such changes.

In the observed rural areas and schools the scope to move seemed to be generally highest for students with high economic backgrounds and/or high grades and lack of these forms of capital was a major potential obstacle, as was the newly arrived students' lack of fluency in Swedish, which they required to connect to local groups and be part of the society. The local community, pupils and teachers have done what they can to help the new arrivals to cope in school, learn the language and seize educational opportunities, but language difficulties are still raised as the main impediments to educational success.

We also found some family connections and kinship extending far back in time are often referred to, so it might be hard for a newcomer to exert any kind of influence and participate in such societies where relations are built up across time and it is important to know 'your place'. However, this seemed to be most difficult initially, according to teachers who had moved into the places long ago.

Moreover, the newly arrived students commented that the teachers cared about them, and that both the places and schools were safe and calm. Some of our data also show that other students tried to take care of, and protect, the newly arrived studentsand that there was a strong emotional dimension of this form of capital, in accordance with extensions of Bourdieu's ideas by some feminist researchers. For example, Reay (2004) recognises emotional capital in the form of emotionally valued assets and skills. This kind of emotional capital seems to be important in relation to the local micropolitics of new migration found in our data.

Further, the newly arrived could also develop some form of symbolic capital, e.g. through success in sport. This could also (presumably) have emotional dimensions, given the passions aroused by football, which facilitates participation and increases chances to be a part of the society. In sum, both social and symbolic capital are important for participation, but they take time for (all) newcomers to develop. In addition, all forms of capital affect the available options and social relations of individuals and groups within and between areas, which shift at multiple levels over time. Massey (1994) uses the concept of power geometry rather than the Bourdieusian concepts of field, habitus and capital. We attribute this at least partly to her background as a historical materialist and cultural geographer, but she also noted that when various social groups and individuals become mobile the reasons are often strongly entwined with the economy and influenced by power relations:

> There are differences in the degree of movement and communication, but also in the degree of control and initiation. (Massey, 1994, p. 151)

The contemporary final report from the Swedish parliamentary countryside committee raises the specific importance of both asylum seekers and new arrivals for future rural development in this sense too, and states that 'Successful integration of asylum seekers and new arrivals is of the utmost importance for the future development of many countryside communities' (SOU, 2017:1, s 23). That people with high levels of capital have tended to leave the focal rural areas and refugees and asylum seekers have moved in may actually be part of a deliberate national long-term political strategy.

Flows of goods, capital and people are highly significant for the development of geo-social spaces as they play major roles in the reciprocal constitution of society and spaces within them. Hence, the recent immigration into Sweden has affected all parts of society, but the school system may have shouldered the greatest responsibility for the immigrants' integration (Nilsson and Bunar, 2016). This certainly seems to apply to the six rural regions we investigated, where generally (as shown by our data) there has been very little advance warning or chance to prepare for the new arrivals. Clearly there are needs to consider carefully the power relations, capital and demographic changes in the rural areas, as well as their impacts on both the places and schools, to assist the required integration and participation. There have been positive outcomes already, albeit on a small scale. Better planning and stronger resourcing of recipient regions would be a worthy political investment that should provide significant benefits for individuals and communities. Education should be given important consideration in these respects. The young people who moved in have expressed positive views of the rural places and sometimes also desires to stay in them. This is encouraging. However, for staying to be a viable option (for both new and old local students) there are needs to increase the availability of education, work opportunities, public transport and various other services. A conclusion is that the unbalanced power-geometry between different parts of Sweden obstructs the development of a sense of place and space built on mutual history and kinship. Metrocentric political oligarchies and their policies relating to demographic change, which hinder mutuality, are problematic, particularly recent market-political varieties, which leave both old and new locals quite alone at the mercy of market investors and without support from a national political level.

References

Argent, N. (2016). Demographic change. Beyond the urban-rural divide, in M. Shucksmith and D. L. Brown (Eds.), *Routledge International Handbook of Rural Studies*, 29-35, London and New York: Routledge.

Beach, D. (2017). Whose justice is this! Capitalism, class and education justice and inclusion in the Nordic countries: race, space and class history, *Education Review*, 69(5): 620-637

Beach, D, From, T, Johansson, M and and Öhrn, E. (2018). Educational and spatial justice in rural and urban areas in three Nordic countries: A meta-ethnographic analysis. *Education Inquiry,* 9(1): 4-21.

Balfour, R., Mitchell, C. and Moletsane, R. (2008). Troubling contexts: toward a generative theory of rurality as education research. *Journal of Rural and Community Development*, 3(3): 95-107.

Bourdieu, P. (1987). What makes a social class? On the theoretical and practical existence of groups. *Berkley Journal of Sociology*. Keynote address to the Dean's Symposium on "Gender, Age, Ethnicity and Class: Analytical Constructs or Folk Categories?" at The University of Chicago, April 9-10, 1987. Translated from French by Loic J. D. Wacquant and David Young.

Callewaert, S. (1996) Pierre Bourdieu, in H. Andersen and L B Kaspersen (Eds.) *Klassisk och modern samhällsteori* [Classic and modern theory of Social Science], 363—383, Lund: Studentlitteratur.

Fjellman, A-M., Yang Hansen, K and Beach, D. (2018). School choice and implications for equity: the new political geography of the Swedish upper secondary school market, *Educational Review*. 71(4): 518-539

Hargreaves, L, Kvalsund, R and Galton, M. (2009). Reviews of research on rural schools and their communities in British and Nordic countries: Analytical perspectives and cultural meaning. *International Journal of Educational Research*, 48(2): 80-88.

Harvey, D. (1996). *Justice, nature and the geography of difference: A meta-theory for ecological socialists?* Oxford: Blackwell.

Hedberg and Haandrikman. (2014). Repopulation of the Swedish countryside: Globalisation by international migration. *Journal of Rural Studies* (34): 128-138.

Hedlund, M., Carson, D. A., Eimermann, M. and Lundmark, L. (2017). Repopulating and revitalising rural Sweden? Re-examining immigration as a solution to rural decline. *Geographical Journal* 183(4): 400-413.

Holm, A-S. (2008). *Relationer i skolan. En studie av femininiteter och maskuliniteter i år 9.* [Relations in school. A study of femininities and masculinities in the 9th grade, in Swedish with an English summary]. Thesis. Gothenburg: Acta Universitatis Gothoburgensis.

Johansson, M (2017) 'Yes, the power is in the town': An ethnographic study of student participation in a rural Swedish secondary school. *Australian and International Journal of Rural Education* 27(2): 61-76.

Lgr 11 (2018). *Curriculum for the compulsory school, preschool class and school-age educare* [Läroplan för grundskolan, förskoleklass och fritidshem]. Stockholm: Skolverket

Massey, D. (1994). *Space, place and gender*. Cambridge: Polity Press.

Nilsson, J and Bunar, N. (2016). Educational responses to newly arrived students in Sweden: Understanding the struture and influence of post-migration ecology. *Scandinavian Journal of Educational Research*, 60(4): 399-416.

Öhrn, E and Weiner, G. (2007). Urban education in Europe: section editors' introduction, W T Pink and G W Noblit (Red), *International handbook of urban education*. Dordrecht: Springer.

Reay, D. 2004. "Gendering Bourdieu's Concepts of Capitals? Emotional Capital, Women and Social Class." *The Sociological Review* 52: 57-74.

Rönnlund, M and Tollefsen, A. (2016). *Rum. Samhällsvetenskapliga perspektiv.* [Space. Perspective from social science]. Stockholm: Liber.

Rosvall, P-Å. (2017). Understanding career development amongst immigrant youth in a rural place. *Intercultural Education*. 28(6): 523-542.

Rye, J F. (2006). Rural youths' images of the rural. *Journal of Rural Studies* 22(4): 409-421.

Sernhede, O. (2007). Territorial stigmatisation. Hip Hop and informal schooling, in W T Pink and G W Noblit (Eds.), *International handbook of urban education.* Dordrecht: Springer.

Shucksmith, M. (2012). Class, Power and Inequality in Rural Areas: Beyond Social Exclusion? *Sociologia Ruralis*, 52(4): 377-396.

Shucksmith, M. (2018). Re-imagining the rural: From rural idyll to Good Countryside. *Journal of Rural Studies*, Vol 59: 163-172.

Shucksmith, M and Brown, D L. (2016). Framing Rural Studies in the Global North, in M. Shucksmith and D. L. Brown, (Eds.), *Routledge International Handbook of Rural Studies*, 1-26, London and New York: Routledge.
Solstad, K J. (2009). The impact of globalisation on small communities and small schools in Europe, i T Lyons, J-Y Choi and G McPhan (Eds.), *Proceedings from international symposium for innovation in rural education,* University of New England, Australia.
Sørensen, N U and Pless, M. (2017). Living on the periphery of youth. Young people's narratives of youth life in rural areas. *Young*, 25(4S): 1S-17S.
SOU (2017). *För Sveriges landsbygder—en sammanhållen politik för arbete, hållbar tillväxt och välfärd.* [For the Swedish countryside—a coherent politic for work, sustainability and welfare] SOU 2017: 1 and 2. Näringslivsdepartementet.
SOU (2008). *Mångfald som möjlighet— Åtgärder för ökad integration på landsbygden.* [Pluralism as a possibility—Activities for increased integration in the countryside] SOU 2008:56. Näringslivsdepartementet.
Statistic Sweden. (2018). *Flyttningar efter region, ålder och kön. År 1997—2017* [Migration based on regions, age and sex]. http://www.statistikdatabasen.scb.se/pxweb/sv/ssd/ START__BE__BE0101__BE0101J/Flyttningar97/?rxid=71dc4093-7169-42e6-84e6-0d7b9c27a5c3 [2018-04-10]
Stenbacka, J. (2011). Othering the rural: About the construction of rural masculinities and the unspoken urban hegemonic ideal in Swedish media. *Journal of Rural Studies*. Volume 27 (3): 235-244.
Stenbacka, S. (2012). "The rural" intervening in the lives of internal and international migrants: migrants, biographies and translocal practices, in C. Hedberg and R. M. do Carmo (Eds.), *Translocal ruralism*. Netherlands: Springer: 55-72.
Stockdale, A.(2004). Rural Out-Migration: Community Consequences and Individual Migrant Experiences. *Sociologia Ruralis*, 44(2): 167-194.
Svenska Dagbladet (2017 July 4). *Klyftan mellan stad och land* ökar [The gap between the city and countryside is increasing. Retrieved from https://www.svd.se/klyftan-okar-mellan-stad-och [2017-08-15].
Svensson, L. (2010). Var du bor spelar roll— landsort eller storstad. [Where you live matters—countryside or big city, in Swedish]. In: Ungdomsstyrelsen (Ed), *Fokus 01. En analys av ungas inflytande*. Stockholm: Ungdomsstyrelsen.
Swedish Migration Agency. (2015). Årsredovisning 2015 [Annual report 2015]. Stockholm Migrationsverket.
Swedish Migration Agency. (2017). Årsredovisning 2017 [Annual report 2017]. Stockholm Migrationsverket.
Swedish Schools Inspectorate. (2014). *Utbildning för nyanlända elever* [Education for newly arrived pupils]. Stockholm: Skolinspektionen.
Swedish Schools Inspectorate. (2016). *Skolinspektionens årsrapport 2016.* [Annual report of the Swedish Schools Inspectorate 2016] Stockholm: Skolinspektionen.

Chapter 6

Reproduction of social relations in rural schools and communities

Maria Rönnlund and Per-Åke Rosvall

Introduction

A general conclusion drawn from the *Rural youth* project is that social relations and divisions are seldom explicitly discussed, exposed or acknowledged either in teaching situations or in everyday communication in the rural schools. However, as previous chapters have indicated, they are implicitly expressed in various ways in everyday life, in both practice and discourse. In this chapter we further describe and discuss these indications. Drawing on previous analyses and some new ones, we discuss how social relations are manifested in discourses and practices related to the everyday school life and wider social life of the rural places. We focus particularly on some of the issues discussed in previous chapters that relate to gender and social class.[1] Two such issues are *who* and *what* is represented in the pedagogic practices in the researched rural schools (see also chapter three). Another is the influence of social class and gender on the extent of restriction and freedom of choices in, for example, leisure-time activities (see also chapter two), education and career (see also chapter four). For example, we discuss gender and class dimensions of the prominence, recognition and prestige of certain activities in school and public discourse, and various ways in which social class was locally expressed.

As elsewhere throughout this book, we apply a spatial perspective when analysing social relations and divisions. Thus, we consider the context of social relations and divisions that we observed or emerged during the research. The analysis draws on a relational understanding that social relations and space create each other—gender and class have spatial expressions, but social relations and structures are also created by space itself. As argued by Massey (1994, p. 87): 'Those unequal class relations do not, as the saying goes, exist on the head of a pin. They are organised spatially.' And this also applies to gender relations. The physical environment and social relations that intersect the local are essential constituents of a place. However, the characteristics of a local area need to be

---

1. As immigrant background has been thoroughly discussed in chapter five, we focus here on social relations related to gender and social class.

understood in relation to both its internal social relations and external relations. 'The identity of a place does not derive from some internalised history. It derives from, in large part, precisely from the specificity of its interactions with "the outside"' (Massey, 1994, p. 169). This implies that a place should be understood in relation to, for example, the dominant gender relations in society and 'the wider structures of capitalist economy' (ibid., p. 89). In order to integrate space and spatiality with gender and social class in our analysis, we pay attention to two (discourse and practice) spatial layers of the focal rural areas and schools.

After a brief overview of research on gender and class dimensions of rural youths' lives, we present our analysis in two sections, entitled, 'Social relations in teaching practices and everyday school life' and 'Social relations in rural social life'. The chapter closes with a discussion and concluding comments.

Gender and class in previous research on rural youth

Research on youth living in rural areas (life and educational conditions, transitions and everyday life etc.) clearly presents the gender relations as more distinct, with more fixed femininities and masculinities, than those encountered and navigated by youth in urban areas (cf. Härnsten, Holmstrand, Lundmark, Hellsten, Rosén and Lundström, 2005). However, variations in rural places have also been discerned—they are reportedly gendered and classed in various ways and have different gender and class structures (e.g. Allen and Hollingworth, 2013; Forsberg and Stenbacka, 2013). These variations in social relations influence young people's experiences of everyday life and life paths. For example, there are differences in ways in which young men and women in rural environments tend to use their local environments and gain access to social networks, which affects both the activities they engage in, and the depth of involvement they feel (e.g. Waara, 1996; 2011). In an illustrative study, young men in rural Danish areas evaluated their social relations and opportunities for leisure and entertainment activities more positively than young women, and more frequently agreed that they had a lot in common with other people of their age in the area (Bloksgaard, Thidemann and Hansen, 2015). In addition, research from Sweden indicates that rural girls talk more about moving to urban settings and education being a way to achieve this (Öhrn, Asp-Onsjö and Holm, 2017; Sandell, 2007).

Social class has received less attention than gender in studies on rural youth, and is less intensively analysed in rural contexts than in urban contexts. We assume this is at least partly because class positions are more blurred and more difficult to decide and identify in rural contexts than in urban ones. For example, in rural contexts working sometimes involve being a Jack of all trades, perhaps running a farm and/or engaging in other types of entrepreneurial business and various kinds of seasonal jobs. Moreover, in a Swedish context, social class seems to be less visible than gender in rural environments. For example, housing and school segregation and school choices tend to be less distinct and clear than in urban areas (Bunar and Ambrose, 2016). Consequently, perceptions of *we* and the *others within* rural places are not always obvious, except when *we* refers to rural people and *they* to people living in urban areas (see for example chapter five). Detailed explorations of these issues indicate that class, and ethnicity, are more central categorisations for youths in metropolitan schools than in rural schools (Öhrn, 2012). Some indicate that family background is an important element of social relations in rural areas (Holm, 2008), and that class and ethnicity can be expressed through talk about family background. However, as mentioned above, social class has received relatively little attention in research on rural youth, so its importance in everyday rural life is unclear.

Following this brief review of earlier research, we turn our attention to manifestations of gender and social class in our data, as noted in both previous analyses and further analyses presented here, highlighting aspects of social relations where gender and class apparently play prominent roles.

Social relations in teaching practices and everyday school life

Both social class and gender were seldom explicitly addressed and discussed in the teaching and everyday school life we observed. Nevertheless, as discussed below, social relations were implicitly expressed in practice and discourse during the school day through the gendering of certain activities and making male-associated activities more prestigious than female-associated activities. Furthermore, social relations and social orders were expressed in dichotomous notions of *centrum* and periphery.

The greater prominence of male-associated activities

In this section we highlight how the local place and local life was represented in teaching and what *within* the local that was represented most frequently and strongly. We focus in particular in teaching episodes about working life and the local labour market. In Sweden, working life and the local labour market are regarded as key areas of knowledge in the school subject of social science (Swedish National Agency for Education, Lgr 11). The aim is to ensure that the students learn about key aspects of labour markets, working life conditions and environments, employment and relevant regulations as well as educational pathways, career choices and entrepreneurship in a global society. Furthermore, social science teaching should cover relationships between socioeconomic background, education, housing and welfare. In addition, although this is less explicitly stated in curricula, it should cover relationships between socioeconomic background and positions in labour markets as well as effects of these relationships on gender and other forms of (in)equality (Swedish National Agency for Education, Lgr 11).

When analysing how working life and local labour markets were represented in teaching practices, we found a tendency for traditionally male-associated occupations and workplaces to receive more space and attention in teaching content than female-associated occupations and workplaces. For example, in one of the schools, students were taught about the local history of mining and forestry work, while local health and care labour was seldom raised.

Giving more attention to traditionally male-associated occupations applied particularly to the schools that did not offer short work experience periods (PRAO, see chapter four) at a workplace as part of the education about working life and labour markets, and had replaced the direct experiences offered through PRAO by oral representations about the local labour market in combination with organised study visits at local work places. The study visits we participated in took place at work-places where many men worked and they were guided by men, for example a garage and the department for rescue, fire preparedness and crisis at the municipal office. As a consequence, work places where many men worked were given more attention than work places like the local residential home or the local preschool where many women worked. Also in the classroom there was a tendency to give more attention to men's work, occupations and workplaces. The students also strongly contributed to this pattern themselves:

Teacher: Do you know what an entrepreneur is?
Boy: Someone running his own business.
Teacher: Yes, that's right. Let's reflect on that together. If you're an entrepreneur, what's your working day like?
Girl: One might work at home.
Boy: You work when you feel like it.
Boy: My dad has a company.

Boy:	And my dad had a shop when we lived in [...]. He had to work a lot with invoices and stuff. I know what life as an entrepreneur was like for him, but I don't know what it's like for others.
Teacher:	That's right, it depends on what you're doing. Continue to reflect, what may a working day be like for an entrepreneur?
Boy:	It can be long.
Teacher:	[addresses one boy whose parents run a farm] You should know what a working day's like,
Boy:	You need to come up with ideas'
Other students join in:	
Boy:	To be very motivated
Girl:	Initiative.
Girl:	Creative. (Inland School, October 20)

In the lesson that followed, the teacher arranged a study visit to the local garage, owned and led by a male businessman. During the lesson after the study visit, the teacher followed it up by saying:

Teacher:	You met Peter during the study visit on Friday, how is he, do you think? Do you find him creative?
Boys and girls:	Yes.
Boy:	He's the best.
Girl:	He's creative. (Inland School, November 2)

During this series of lessons, traditional male occupations and work places that attract many men were given more attention than traditional female coded occupations and work places. Considering the teaching about entrepreneurship, there was also a tendency to pay more attention to male businessmen and male entrepreneurs, although there were obviously also female entrepreneurs operating locally.

The teaching also addressed historically and traditionally masculine activities such as hunting, forestry and fishing more often than female-associated activities such as handicraft, cooking and caring, a pattern previously highlighted by Gustafsson and Öhrn (2012). This was particularly apparent in schools in sparsely populated areas. In all theses schools hunting was referred to as part of rural people's livelihood, as a prominent cultural and social activity in local adult society, and as having substantial economic importance. The students learnt to consider the value of activities such as moose hunting in material, i.e. financial, terms (cf. Beach, From, Johansson and Öhrn, 2018). In Mountain School, for example, moose hunting was often presented in teaching content as a traditional local activity and important source of income, but also from other perspectives. The example below, demonstrates how it was integrated in teaching in the subject biology:

> The teacher continues that in the next lesson they will start a new theme in biology. 'We'll dissect a moose's head. We'll start with the eyes and then continue with the brain.' (Mountain School, November 12)

However, the main pattern in the teaching was to emphasise hunting as a cultural tradition and as a source of income. The focus was on its contribution to the local economy, and much less attention was paid to often female labour related to hunting such as light-butchery processes.

Regarding education more generally, we also found examples of male-associated activities gaining more attention than corresponding female-associated activities. For example, in River there were long-established orientations in the upper secondary programmes to attract boys through sports activities: there was a social science programme in which optional courses included ice hockey training. Theoretically a girl could choose such course and play with boys but it had not happened to date and nor did we overhear any of the girls discussing it as an option. Furthermore, there was no equivalent option associated with sports that traditionally attract females, although there was a strong interest among girls in the region for a programme with optional dance courses. After petitioning and expressing their opinions to local politicians the municipality office decided to introduce such a programme. However, it is worth noting that the girls said both during classroom observations and in interviews that while they had to argue and fight for a dance programme, their opinion was that the boys were *given* an ice-hockey programme, without even having asked for one.

In the next section we demonstrate how social relations and orders were expressed in discourse and practice through the dichotomous notion of centre-periphery.

Social division based on centre-periphery

In the six rural schools we studied, virtually all the youths of the surrounding region, including those living in small villages quite far from the local centre where the school was located, attended the same school, and a noticeable social divide that appeared in the data was between young people living in the local centre where the school was located and those living outside the local centre. This was a discursive practice that appeared in all six municipalities, but was clearest in the de/industrial areas. In River School, it was also something that permeated the daily practice, as students living in the town centre and those living in the villages outside were placed in separate classes. This was not done in any of the other schools where there were sufficient students to have more than one school class for each age group. However, the division was still recognised in practice also in these schools, as an effect of distances and the need for transport to and from school for students living in outer villages. Students who were dependent on the municipality's school shuttle usually came to school earlier than those who could walk to school, and thus waited for the first lesson to start together, and had to wait (together) after the school day for the school bus. This made them spend time together and socialise both while waiting for and during transport to and from school.

Another pattern that emerged from the data was the strength of the centre-periphery dichotomy in self-identification and discourse. Residence in the centre of the municipality where the school was located or outside the centre was clearly an identity marker for many of the young people we met, and one of the first things they mentioned about themselves. In River School this was especially apparent, for example as in the interview below where Reine immediately clearly stated that he was not from the local centre of River:

Interviewer: Could you describe what it's like to live here?
Reine: You know, I'm not from here. I'm from a place 20 kilometres from here.   (River School, April 20)

The verbal positioning in relation to the centre-periphery scale made obvious that students who came from villages outside the central place more often understood themselves as *rural* than those living where the school was located, for example expressed in phrases such as I like 'I come from the sticks'.

Geo-spatial markers also underlay some teachers' understanding and descriptions of the students. Notably, some teachers claimed that students living in small villages outside the centre where the school was located had less motivation to study than their peers living in the centre. This was because their parents generally had a low educational background and they did not need good educational qualifications for their future plans:

Teacher: The motivation to study is not great in the villages, there they prefer driving snowmobiles and horse riding, and want to stick with that, they just want to stay there, taking over the farm.
(Coastal School, March 12)

In summary, the teachers seldom explicitly touched on social class in the classroom. However, their comments about students' parents' occupations and educational background, and their general attitude towards students from the *centre* and *periphery* in terms of motivation to study and future plans implicitly referred to a social distinction not just a space-geographical one between the students.

Social relations in rural social life

As observed in school, class and gender were rarely addressed and discussed in everyday conversations outside school. Even when students and teachers were directly asked questions about social divisions based on class and gender, such divisions were not acknowledged. For example, social class was mostly treated as a phenomenon of big cities than of rural places, where everybody was understood to belong to the same community (see chapter two). This was a strong discourse, and as shown in previous chapters, only problematised and questioned to a low extent among the youths themselves. However, as we will elaborate in more detail below—socio-spatial relations and divisions based on gender and social class were certainly present.

Local activities—mainly discussed as men's activities

Both boys and girls (and female and male adults) participated in traditional, often transgenerational, activities that inhabitants of the rural places associated with the local places (snowmobiling, fishing, hunting etc.). However, even though both boys and girls participated in these activities, there was a general tendency to talk about the local activities as men's interests/activities. The primary manifestation of this was that male individuals (friends, family members, relatives, neighbours etc.) were usually mentioned when discussing fishing, hunting and sports activities etc. An Inland School boy provided an illustrative quotation: 'I fish a lot with my dad, he's a fishing enthusiast, he loves to fish [...] we used to go on fishing trips together.' In a second illustrative quotation, another boy from Inland town talked about hunting, and as he only mentioned male hunting companions, the interviewer asked if his mother did not participate:

> *Interviewer:* You mentioned hunting and fishing, and your grandfather and father.
> *Jacob:* Actually my father doesn't hunt, but my grandfather does.
> *Interviewer:* What about your mother then? Isn't she interested in hunting and fishing?
> *Jacob:* No, she's more into cooking and stuff, cooking the meat.
> (Inland School, October 22)

Another factor that contributed to the discourse about local activities (snowmobiling, fishing, hunting etc.) being mainly masculine was that certain male-associated practices connected to these activities received much more attention in everyday narrations than female-associated practices. There was also a tendency to assign the male-associated elements a higher value. This can be demonstrated by narrations about hunting, such as the following quotation of a girl in Mountain School who had just shot her first moose:

> [The girl picks up her phone, shows a photo and continues...] 'Look here, that's my mom taking out the stomach. And you know my brother's so jealous that I shot a moose before him.' (Mountain School, November 10)

The quotation indicates that the stalking and shooting elements of hunting were more highly valued activities and given more attention in discourse than taking care of hunted animals' bodies, e.g. 'taking out the stomach' or preparing food from the meat ('cooking and stuff', as mentioned in a previous quotation).

Other examples of certain practices connected to local activities being more valued were provided by differences in ways that girls and boys narrated, contextualised and positioned themselves and their female and male friends in relation to snowmobiling. Snowmobiling in a typically *male* manner—tinkering and driving fast—was given most attention in public discourse. The girls' interest in snowmobiling was discursively constructed rather as a *family thing*, and the snowmobile as a means for transporting during excursions to natural sites. In contrast, boys' interest in snowmobiling was discursively constructed as an individual interest in motors, and driving fast. In their talk, boys were represented as active agents in relation to snowmobiling and girls as more passive agents, who had been socialised into the activity through their families, as encapsulated by one of the girls saying, 'This is how I grew up.' The expression reinforces the discourse about snowmobiling and hunting as interests young women learn from their families and incorporate as their own interests, but not fully as active agents (Rosvall, Rönnlund and Johansson, 2018).

Despite the fact that both women and men, girls and boys participated in local traditional activities such as hunting, snowmobiling and similar activities, the predominant discursive practices contributed to the idea of local traditional activities as mainly male activities. And when women's and girls' participation was included discursively, it tended to be described in more passive ways than boys' participation. For example, a teacher in Coastal School talked about driving snow mobiles and motoring as *boys' interests* even though girls in the classes he taught obviously did drive snow mobiles. There were also examples of talking about girls' participation as a hang-around activity:

Interviewer: What do the young people living here do outside school?
Teacher assistant: Sports, snowmobiling, motoring.
Interviewer: And are you referring to girls too?
Teacher assistant: They hang out with the boys.
(Coastal School, February 5)

Thus, despite the indications from our fieldwork that both male and female local inhabitants including boys and girls we interviewed participated in traditional local activities, these activities were often represented as mainly male activities and within them girls were portrayed as having less agency than the boys.

Social class less apparent than in urban environments—but still there

As indicated in previous chapters, social class was an important social divider that was expressed in various ways in discourse and practice, thereby influencing the rural youths' lives. This is a well-documented phenomenon in research on urban youth. For example, social class has been shown to be manifested in young people's career aspirations and school-to-work transitions (Allen and Hollingworth, 2013; Tolonen, 2005). More specifically, urban studies indicate that young people's education and occupations tend to be consistent with the material and structural conditions under which they grew up (see also Beach and Puaca, 2014). Working-class young people (e.g. children of low-ranking officials, craft-oriented small entrepreneurs with little academic education and manual workers) tend to choose similar types of occupation to their parents and thus orient towards vocational education and training. In contrast, young people from middle-class environments with highly-educated parents tend to orient towards continued academic studies. These socialisation patterns are also reflected in the labour market. Youths whose parents have working class positions in the labour market and low education levels tend to end up with unqualified or low-skilled jobs in the service and care sectors to a greater extent than youths from more privileged backgrounds (e.g. Trondman and Bunar, 2001).

Social relations of class have been less intensively explored in rural contexts. In the rural environments we studied, there were few obvious signs of social class divisions, particularly in the sparsely populated areas. For example, it was difficult to distinguish housing segregation or an obvious *we* and *they* discourse based on class, as identified in urban contexts (cf. Öhrn, 2011). Neither was it easy to discern substantial differences in families' economic resources, for example in how people spent their leisure time. There was not a wide range of organised leisure time activities, such as sports, to choose from so most young people participated in the few activities available. However, as discussed for example in chapter two, students were not equally free or able to participate in organised activities, due to differences in available resources, which provided examples of manifestations of social class in our data. For example, the Forest municipality was big geographically and there was only one football team (solely for boys), so the players had to travel long distances for practice sessions, and even further for matches, as one of the players stated:

> There are quite long distances to everything so, for example, we play football but we can't train many times a week. Because there are such long distances it would be impossible to travel so much every week. It's 150 kilometres between [homes of] the two players who live furthest north and south. (Forest School, May 23)

With such long distances involved, organising transportation to training and games was difficult and expensive for some parents, who could not afford to let their children participate. Thus, class, spatial factors (distances) and socio-economic conditions interactively influenced access to activities, and strongly limited some students' possibilities to participate in favoured activities (cf. Johansson, 2017).

Class was also mirrored in the students' study and career choices within the rural places, for example in their choices of upper secondary programmes (see chapter four). This was particularly apparent in municipalities with no upper secondary schools. Students whose parents lacked sufficient social or economic capital to provide accommodation for them in a city could only choose one of the programmes offered by schools within commuting distance, which markedly limited their choices. In the following excerpt, Ingemar (a student at Inland School) discusses whether he will choose an upper secondary school in a nearby municipality that he could travel to daily by bus or one in the region's big city, which would make daily commuting impossible. The excerpt highlights the interaction of economic and social resources with space, as Ingemar's choice will only be financially feasible with the help of social resources provided by relatives:

Interviewer: What programme will you choose?
Ingemar: Probably computer programming.
Interviewer: And where?
Ingemar: Either in X-town or Å-town. [...]
Interviewer: You mentioned that your sister studies in X-town, is she commuting daily? Is that possible?
Ingemar: No, we've arranged to have an apartment there, and we also have relatives there, an aunt and some others, so my sister lives there during her upper secondary school studies.
Interviewer: So, if you choose X-town, you can also live there during your studies?
Ingemar: Yes.

(Inland School, October 14)

While Ingemar could choose to study in the big city thanks to his family's financial and relational resources, other students' future plans were much more uncertain due to less privileged economic and relational situations (see, for example, the description of Sebastian's situation in chapter four). Thus, the students' families financial resources clearly influenced their study and career choices as they provided opportunities or obstacles for accessing valued options outside the geographically nearest town. Thus, economic resources give some young people opportunities to study in places away from home, but strongly restrict opportunities for others.

Our research, as reported in previous chapters and several articles (Johansson, 2017; Rönnlund, Rosvall and Johansson, 2018; Rosvall, 2017), and studies by other authors (e.g. Kiilakoski, 2016) corroborate these patterns. Many young people are under heavy pressure to move to urban areas due to the paucity of educational and employment opportunities in sparsely populated areas, relative to those offered elsewhere, but this is not feasible for those who lack sufficient capital. The local place's materialised resources in combination with the family's economic and social resources clearly steer individuals' future occupational plans (cf. Kirkpatrick Johnson, Elder and Stern, 2005; Beach et al., 2018).

We also noted that social class influenced how the young people saw themselves, for example how they reflected on and planned for the near future, such as their aspirations, as described in chapter four (see also Allen and Hollingsworth, 2013). For students from families with a low education level who wanted to stay in the local place after completing upper secondary school, it seemed important to orient themselves towards an occupation that fitted into the local context, and not to challenge the local social structures. Their parents' education and occupations were important influences on them. They chose progammes and considered future occupations in harmony with their parents' positions in the labour market and general characteristics of the local labour market. This indicates that classed and gendered practices that characterised the rural places formed a local social *culture* that influenced how individual students' reflected on the future.

However, the students themselves did not talk about their social relationships, life conditions and future plans as related to class. Neither was talk about identification connected to social class. They expressed identification with the local place they lived in, and indicated that family relations were important for their sense of belonging and well-being (chapter two; see also Rönnlund, 2019). As argued in other studies, in rural areas family relations over generations are considered to be more visible and often take precedence over class, which seems to be a more abstract category. People in the local area know whose daughter or son you are, and even who your grandparents are, and these identifications are used in different situations to explain and talk about educational and social differences rather than social class (Holm, 2008; Beach et al., 2018). This kind of identification was also characteristic of the students we met, as illustrated by the following quotation:

Karolina: You know, I have all my family here. My grandfather worked at the local food store, he worked there all his life, and now my dad has taken over the store.
Interviewer: So, when you say your last name, everyone knows who you are?
Karolina: Yes, Peter's daughter.
Interviewer: And how do you feel about that?
Karolina: I like it. (Coastal School, February 2)

A general impression was that it seemed easier to understand ones' life and positioning locally in terms of family relations than in sociological dimensions such as class and gender. Another discourse marginalising class and gender relations was the discourse on individualism—talk about and understanding of life conditions, life paths, study and career choices etc. as individual choices, rather than as related to gender, class and place (see chapter four).

Discussion

This chapter focuses on manifestations of social relations of various kinds, relations that, as our analyses (presented both here and other chapters of the book) indicate, play major roles in lives of rural youths. Drawing on a socio-spatial understanding of space and social relations as intrinsically creating each other (cf. Massey, 1994), we conclude that social relations worked as *organising principles* (cf. Rönnlund, 2015) in all six rural environments, albeit with variations both within and among the areas. For example, social class was manifested in the scope of choices available to individual students for leisure-time activities, educational programmes and careers. The centre-periphery relation also worked as a social marker and constructed social distinctions in the rural environments. It was an important element of both students' self-understandings and some teachers' understandings of individual students' academic orientation and likely life trajectories. Furthermore, social class was expressed discursively in talk about students' self-reflections, and (consistently with conclusions regarding other aspects of rural youths' lives reported in other chapters) in terms of ownership and control of spaces, resources and people.

Thus, the analyses presented here and in other chapters emphasise that social relations, space and place influence, powerfully and interactively, young people's lives and that general social societal orders have local expressions. As argued by Massey (1994, p. 23): 'spatial form and geographical location are themselves significant in forming the character of particular social strata'. The locally situated social relations, in turn, mirrored a general social order, indicating that the social relations of the local places interacted with *the outside*—with dominant societal gender relations and the wider structures of global capitalist economy (Massey, 1994, p. 89). All municipalities in the project, regardless of type in terms of rurality, place-bound gender and/or class relations, were struggling with a continuously lower range of services and educational institutions in combination with long distances to places providing such services. These unequal spatial relations that affected everyday lives of the young people living in these rural regions.

Overall, expressions of social categories recorded in our research are consistent with those documented in previous research. For instance, the students' talk about local leisure-time activities revealed transgenerational patterns indicating that participation in common local activities provided access to transgenerational social communities and networks. Through participation in hunting teams, and fishing, motoring and snowmobiling associations, these young people became part of inter-generational, often male-dominated, social networks (Waara, 2011; Bloksgaard et al., 2015). They also accumulated 'location-specific capital' (Moilanen, 2012): a kind of situated social knowledge of demonstrated importance for feeling a sense of belonging to the local community (see also Rönnlund, 2019). According to our observations and respondents, both girls and boys participated in local male-associated activities, which means that our analyses thus indicate there to be less gender stereotyped patterns than in previous studies (e.g. Härnsten et al., 2005). However, the activities were generally dicursively represented as male activities in ways that contributed to a marginalisation of girls' and women's activities.

The analyses presented here and in previous chapters highlight the importance of taking social relations and divisions as well as spatial dimensions into account in analyses of rural youth, life and education. Such perspectives are crucial in order to enhance knowledge about the everyday life of youth.

References

Allen, K. and Hollingworth, S., (2013) 'Sticky subjects' or 'cosmopolitan creatives'? Social class, place and urban young people's aspirations for work in the knowledge economy, *Urban Studies*, 50(3): 499-517.

Beach, D. and Puaca, G., (2014) Changing higher education by converging policy-packages: Education choices and student identities, *European Journal of Higher Education*, 4(1): 67-79.

Beach, D., From, T., Johansson, M., and Öhrn, E., (2018) Educational and spatial justice in rural and urban areas in three Nordic countries: a meta-ethnographic analysis, *Education Inquiry*, 9(1): 4-21.

Beach, D., Johansson, M., Öhrn, E., Rönnlund, M., and Rosvall, P.-Å., (2018) Rurality and education relations: Metro-centricity and local values in rural communities and rural schools. *European Educational Research Journal*.

Bloksgaard, L., Thidemann S., and Hansen, C., (2015) Young in a global context: Gender, mobility and belonging in north Denmark, in S. Faber Thiedeman and H. Pristed Nielsen (Eds.), *Remapping gender, place and mobility: Global confluences and local particularities in Nordic peripheries*, 191-126. Surrey: Ashgate.

Bunar, N. and Ambrose, A., (2016) Schools, choice and reputation: Local school markets and the distribution of symbolic capital in segregated cities. *Research in Comparative and International Education*, 11(1): 34-51.

Forsberg, G. and Stenbacka, S., (2013) Mapping gendered ruralities. *European Countryside*, 1: 1-20.

Gustafsson, J. and Öhrn, E., (2012) *Gender, achievement and place: Boys and masculinities in a rural area*, Paper presented at Aare, Sydney 2-6 December.

Härnsten, G., Holmstrand, L., Lundmark, E., Hellsten, J.-O., Rosén, M. and Lundström, E., (2005) *Vi sätter genus på agendan: Ett deltagarorienterat projekt om flickor och pojkar i glesbygd*. [We are putting gender on the agenda: A participatory oriented project on girls and boys in sparsely populated areas]. Pedagogisk kommunikation nr 6. Växjö university: Pedagogiska institutionen.

Johansson, M., (2017) "Yes, the power is in the town": An ethnographic study of student participation in a rural Swedish secondary school. *Australian and International journal of Rural Education*, 27(2): 61-77.

Kiilakoski, T., (2016) *I am fire but my environment is the lighter: A study on locality, mobility and youth engagement in the Barents region*. Finnish Youth Research Network, Internet publications 98.

Kirkpatrick Johnson, M., Elder, G. H. and Stern, M., (2005) Attachments to family and community and the young adult transition of rural youth. *Journal of Research on Adolescence*. 15: 99-125.

Lgy11., (2011) *Läroplan för gymnasieskolan* [Lgy11 Curriculum for Upper Secondary School]. Stockholm: Swedish National Board of Education.

Massey, D., (1994) *Space, place and gender*. Cambridge: Polity press.

Moilanen, M., (2012) Job is where the heart Is? An analysis of geographical labour mobility among young adults, in U-D. Bæck and G. Paulgaard (Eds.) *Rural futures? Finding one's place within changing labour markets*, 83-102.

Holm, A-S., (2008) *Relationer i skolan. En studie av femininiteter och maskuliniteter i år 9*. Diss. Göteborg: Acta Universitatis Gothoburgensis.

Öhrn, E., (2011) Class and ethnicity at work. Segregation and conflict in a Swedish secondary school, *Education Inquiry*, 2(2), 345-357.

Öhrn, E., (2012) Urban education and segregation: The responses from young people, *European Educational Research Journal*, 1(1), 45-57.

Öhrn, E., Asp-Onsjö, L. and Holm, A.-S. (2017) Discourses on gender and achievement in lower secondary education, in K. Kantasalmi and G. Holm (Eds), *The State, Schooling and Identity: Diversifying Education in Europe* (p. 173-192). London: Palgrave Macmillan.

Paechter, C., (2009) Response to Mary Lou Rasmussen's 'Beyond gender identity', *Gender and Education*, 21(4): 449-453.

Paechter, C., (2012) Bodies, identities and performances: reconfiguring the language of gender and schooling, *Gender and Education*, 24(2), 229-241.

Rönnlund, M., (2019) 'I love this place, but I won't stay': Identification with place and imagined spatial futures amongst youth living in rural areas in Sweden. *Young*.

Rönnlund, M,. (2015) Schoolyard stories. Processes of gender identity at a 'childrens' place, *Childhood*, 22(1): 85-100.

Rönnlund, M., Rosvall, P.-Å., and Johansson, M., (2018) Vocational or academic track? Study and career plans among Swedish students living in rural areas, *Journal of Youth Studies*, 21(3): 360-375.

Rosvall, P. A., (2017) Understanding career development amongst immigrant youth in a rural place. *Intercultural Education*, 28(6): 523-542.

Rosvall, P. Å., Rönnlund, M., and Johansson, M., (2018) Young people's career choices in Swedish rural contexts: Schools' social codes, migration and resources. *Journal of Rural Studies*, 60: 43-51.

Sandell, A., (2007) *Utbildningssegregation och självsortering. Om gymnasieval, genus och lokala praktiker.* [Segregation and self-sorting in eduction: on choice of upper secondary education, gender and local practices]. Thesis. Malmö University College.

Soja, E. W., (2010) *Seeking spatial justice*. Minneapolis: University of Minnesota Press.

Stenbacka, S., (2011) Othering the rural: About the construction of rural masculinities and the unspoken urban hegemonic ideal in Swedish media, *Journal of Rural Studies* 27: 235-244.

Swedish National Agency for Education., (2016) Uppföljning av gymnasieskolan. Regeringsuppdrag—uppföljning och analys av gymnasieskolan. Stockholm: Skolverket [National Agency for Education]. Follow-up of Upper Secondary School.

Trondman, M., and Bunar, N., (2001) Varken ung eller vuxen. Samhället idag är ju helt rubbat. Stockholm: Atlas.

Waara, P., (2011) Mellan något och någon—forskning om ungdom på landsbygden. [Between something and someone—research about youth in the countryside]. In: P. Möller (Ed), *Vem bygger landet?* Vilnius: Gidlunds förlag.

Chapter 7

Education politics and rural secondary schools

Dennis Beach and Monica Johansson

Deriving from the emergence and expansion of the Swedish elementary Folk School (*Folkskolan*) subsequent to a national law in 1842 (*Folkskolestadgan*), it is the post-war reform of education in Sweden and the creation of the common secondary school (i.e. the common national comprehensive school, *Grundskolan*) that is usually taken as the strongest indicator of Sweden's national commitment to social and educational equality (OECD, 2005; Richardson, 2010). It emerged between 1949 and 1962 from new laws, projects and experiments, to become a common school for all students for new times, but there have always been inconsistencies in terms of the one school for all idea in practice (Richardsson, 2010) and in the course of the *Rural youth* project, we have explored dimensions of this dilemma in six local rural areas.

Analytical themes

As Massey pointed out, identities of place are unfixed, contested, multiple, and culturally and historically produced through a mix of links and interconnections with what lies 'outside or beyond' the local immediate context (Massey, 1994, p. 5). The history and geography of places are very closely related in these respects. Geography deals with lands, oceans, atmosphere, people and cultures with reference to space and place, and history is the study of the past of these lands, oceans, atmospheres, people and cultures. Geography and history set the material, cultural and spatial foundations of places and their identities. They help shape places for the present and the future. The chapter has attempted to draw out and focus on some of the major relevant themes that have emerged from the analyses in the previous chapters in relation to these issues. The first theme is that rural areas, the schools in them, the students that go there, and the relationships (real and present and imaginary and future) that they form with education institutions and their agents to create educational opportunities and experiences are not uniform within, let alone also across rural areas (as seems to be understood by national policy makers), but quite different. As also chapters two and three suggest, there is no one standard form of rurality or rural educational relation or output. Rather this summarising and disfiguring norm is produced and reproduced through metro-centric lenses. The significance of private property is lifted in relation to this with a focus on issues of forms of and access to private capital.

The next theme is connected to the first. It is that despite differences, there are some consistencies with respect to rural education and schools, the people in them, and the educational and life opportunities they create that are not simple metro-centric aberrations and some of them seem to be present in schools and education social relations in urban areas as well. It is the hegemony of private ownership and private value within a current global politics of market governance in education and a general fall in educational performance standards and increasing inequalities in schools (Yang Hansen and Gustafsson, 2018) and between densely and sparsely populated areas (Fjellman, Yang Hansen and Beach, 2018).

Although not dwelt on extensively in the chapters as such, there are two sub-points to consider here. The first is that market politics are now the ubiquitous policy context for and framework of the educational macro level. The second is that market governace has completely failed to live up to the promises made for it by the governments who proposed and introduced it. This applies both nationally (SOU, 2017:35; Yang Hansen and Gustafsson, 2018) and internationally (Verger, Fontdevila, Zancajo, and Steiner-Khamsi, 2016), particularly in rural and poor sub-urban spaces (Åberg-Bengtsson, 2009; Fjellman, 2019). Market governance has not produced a uniformly rich expansion of choice options, national system efficiency and quality improvements of the kind promoted in proposal by the national government (see e.g. Swedish Government Proposition, 1991/91: 95), but rather instead a lack of educational (choice) possibilities for economically subordinated groups in territorially stigmatised 'off-places' in urban areas and in remote rural areas that also strikes unevenly in terms of social class and gender (see chapters three and six).

Although again not extensively dwelt on in the earlier chapters the deterioration of educational quality and equality in Sweden following marketisation is apparent and has also been identified in other works, such as by Östh, Andersson and Malmberg (2013) in relation to school choice and Yang Hansen and Gustafsson (2018), who identified increases in inequities particularly from late 1980 onwards that were distinctly acute in sub-urban spaces and for children from families with a migrant history (Bunar and Ambrose, 2016; Beach, 2017). Increased segregation with respect to student composition and academic outcomes across different schools was found to be a main driver and differential trends in the relationship between family educational background and school outcome between immigrant and non-immigrant sub populations were also indicated. Between-school differences in achievement levels have increased in all regions and school segregation with respect to socio-economic and ethnic composition of students has increased too (Yang Hansen and Gustafsson, 2018).

Five subheadings have been used to organise the five themes and important details within them. They are:

Differences between different types of rural area and their schools;
Rural conditions and an urban political oligarchy;
The significance of private ownership;
Compensatory forms of capital in rural areas and schools;
Structures of support and the mobility imperative.

These side-headings represent themes that have emerged in the analysis for the present chapter, which has broadly taken the form of a meta-ethnographic narrative. This narrative concerns resistances and accommodations to urbanite political hegemony within education systems in rural areas and the conditioning of the conditions for the production of local educational relations in global capitalist political economies and education policy contexts, such as those apparent in Sweden today.

Differences between different types of rural area and their schools

As pointed out in chapters two, three and six there are important differences between different types of rural area and the schools there. But the differences are also ones that exist within a consistent pattern where historical, political and economic investments have pushed cities to grow for decades and where subsequently the number of school places there have grown too, whilst almost half of the country's rural municipalities have smaller populations today than they did just three decades ago (Fjellman et al., 2018). This is of course a feature that is more obvious at upper secondary levels and in relation to higher education (Haley, 2017; Fjellman et al., 2018) but it means thus, when measured in terms of local economy, patterns of national and private investment, and the facilities and access to education resources they create, (a) that students from rural areas are discriminated against in national policies (Åberg Bengtsson, 2009; Östh et al., 2013; Haley, 2017) and that (b) only some of them; i.e. the ones who are committed to and can afford to travel; and are able to guarantee being able to make a choice of the education they desire (Fjellman et al., 2018). It identifies that in rural areas, as also in urban and suburban ones (Beach, 2018; Beach and

Sernhede, 2011), inequalities in terms of education access, use and output tend to become concentrated in certain places and is discussed in chapters one and eight. However, our research discerns not only spatial but also social and capital differences within and among local areas and between rural and urban areas as significant for what becomes of educational policies there (Johansson, 2017).

Rural conditions and an urban political oligarchy

Variations in the identification and critique of metrocentric were communicated by the young people in the different researched areas. These related both to the content of the policies that were addressed, ranging from transport, culture, health and recreation, to education and schooling: although of course particularly educational provisions (elementary, secondary and tertiary education and vocational training) and work opportunities were amongst the points raised most consistently. This is in line with our research focussing on schools mainly and of us talking primarily to students and teachers there about these matters. Variations were found between the places, within the places, and within the regions where our schools are located. Commuting possibilities were considered and were identified as varying between the different places with respect to the average distances between home and school, the quality of road and rail connections, and the availability of effective public transport. In some remote, sparsely populated and poorly connected rural areas there are few educational and vocational options *in situ*, and getting to places where there are more opportunities for various kinds of recreation and entertainment as well as education and work was described as requiring long, time-consuming, and for some also expensive travel.

For some of the young informants physical distance and the time needed to cover it were the main problems. However for others, the problems with physical distances were also linked to criticisms of current politics. They were linked to the lack of a rural perspective in national politics by both staff and students in the schools, and issues such as fuel tax that hit of course particularly hard in rural areas, were taken up in illustration; and the extraction of value from local natural resources and labour power was sometimes also castigated. Anger and frustration were expressed at this too. But there was also some derision in the discourses about cities and the people in them. This came particularly from people in the sparsely populated areas, where Laws such as those regulating hunting and culling were pointed out as causing problems (Johansson, 2017). Some more critical members of the local adult populations, including some members of staff at two of the schools, even discussed the issue of a deliberate politics of marginalisation from Stockholm in terms of conventional *centrum-periphery* relations and even forms of extraction-colonisation within what was occasionally even expressed as a deliberately planned politics:

> We have huge forests and water (rivers) but everything's going south. The forest is made into plywood and the water into power to fuel the south and Stockholm—those are incomes we don't get to share ... They simply disappear from the area ... The left-wing parties have tried to shift taxation revenue to the local councils in places with the water and forests, which would be good for us! But it is utopic (laughs)!
> (Forest School, March 27)

There is definitely an element of exploitation involved in relation to urban-rural relations according to this extract, along with a hint of a feeling concerning a politically legislated form of exploitation colonialism that creates and exploits an economic labour power (and labour force) as a formally underpaid form of labour in the Marxist sense, to extract, refine and transport minerals, other natural products, and refined goods, for the generation of private profit outside the area.

Exploitation colonialism may often include some migration and settlement; such as that connected with the area colonisation of the Sami regions in the North; but what it really involves is the establishment of structures to generate an almost immediate financial gain from the extraction of raw materials through the use of local and imported labour and the refinement of these materials prior or subsequent to transportation from peripheral to more central areas. The examples in the earlier chapters such as chapter two and six relate mainly to the excavation of forests to generate timber to be sawn, milled or pulped, mineral ores to be mined and refined into precious metals or forged into steel, to be later made into ball-bearings, sheet metal, machine and car parts, tools, and so on in other places. They indicate how present conditions extend a situation that was politically engineered in the past and refined (ibid) in ways that are (and increasingly so) geo-historically joined up (Massey, 1994). They are elements of course of class domination and they are clearly visible in the classification and framing of curriculum interactions and educational content in schools, even in the rural areas we have visited, that reflect the ways in the working class has had its history first stolen from it and then repackaged and delivered in competitive arenas as a means to deny opportunities for class consciousness (Maisuria, 2016) and this claim rings true even today, as also chapters five and six have discussed.

This facet is to us something that is deeply ironic. It is part of a historical continuity and connectivity of schooling across history and geographic places. Proletariat labour power and the extraction of raw materials (natural capital) from rural areas has created the economic conditions for fuelling a welfare state education project that has strongly benefitted the new urban middle-, upper-middle classes and produced profits for the upper-class owners and controllers of production of course. But the proletariat effort and the organised *theft* of common value is hidden and disguised (even transfigured) in schools in the dominant class interest within the continuous history of class struggle.

These points have of course been communicated before, such as in the original *Manifesto of the Communist Party* by Karl Marx and Friedrich Engels. In relation to rurality, as they identified there, the bourgeoisie has subjected the country to the rule of towns and has greatly increased the urban population as compared with the rural and it has extracted value from both in the pursuit of economic growth and a profit interest. Lefebvre (2000) made similar notations concerning the politics of (rural and urban) space in the capitalist political economy, when in referring to the German Ideology (by Marx) he identified, as did Marx, that the greatest division of material and mental labour is the separation of town and country, which is described in history books as beginning with (and extending/modernising) the transition from barbarism to civilisation, from tribe to State and from locality to nation, but that runs through the whole history of civilisation to the present day, leading subsequently to the greatest event of the last few decades in terms of the effects of industrialisation on capitalist society and the expansion and effects of urbanism into and in rural areas. As Lefebvre (2000) suggested, industrial capitalism has increasingly organised working life and has greatly expanded its control over private life too, through education relations and possibilities, leisure activities and the political organisation of space and spatial relations.

The significance of private ownership

There are consistencies at the level of the social collectives in both rural and urban areas then, in terms of educational identity, content and relations, that have a long history, and that are connected to the division of labour, and ownership and control of the means of material production (between town and country, between various towns, between branches of production and between manufacturers, commerce and cultural producers), in relation to transport and export of goods (including internationally to different foreign nations) and regarding also the concentration of the population and the creation, reproduction and distribution of forms of capital (Lefebvre, 2000). But there are also obviously then even important differences between, within and because of these divisions, also in each of the rural areas themselves in the project, in terms of educational availabilities, the possibilities that are recognised within them, and the patterns of use and forms of use value that emanate at individual levels (Beach et al., 2018: see also however Corbett, 2015a, 2015b and Stenbacka, 2011). In the following field-note excerpts, from the students Frans and Fanny, describe one example, the value of rural raw materials and the consequences of their distribution from two distinctly different perspectives:

> When I finished the recording Frans carries on talking and speaks of the forest being valuable—there are a lot of people who don't think of that, he says. There's a lot of money if it's privately owned, his maternal grandmother sold half of her forest (400 ha) and got *a lot* of money.
> (Forest School, May 6)

> We have quite nice forest areas here, but they're even nicer down by the main road, so I'll either live down there or here. (…) Or in Germany … My dad (a lorry driver) has been driving there and a lot of exciting things have happened, always something new and exciting and I want to try that too.
> (Forest School, May 4)

For both Frans and Fanny relate positively to the predominant local resource in the area: the forests. But they do this in distinctly different ways. The forest is implied to be owned by one of their respective families (Frans), and for him it might form a resource that could be used in the future to help him travel, study, live and work comfortably in different places thanks to its economic exchange value. In this sense to him the forest owned by his family was an exchangeable resource that if used effectively helped to shrink the restriction of geographic distance and removed barriers for him, to open up educational possibilities as well as cultural experiences and to permit him to valorise his previous learning positively.

For Fanny this exchange value and the possibilities it created were not mentioned. They did not exist in fact for her. The forest was just something of emotional value. It was a nice place to visit and dream about a future in or close to, and parts of it were obviously places she felt drawn to, felt value from, and would like to enjoy the beauty of. Fanny was good student. But the forest was not *property* and thus not a material resource with an economic exchange value that could open up possibilities and cultural experiences in education and social life which would allow her to convert her early educational investments into a useful future capital in the valorisation of a positive identity as a future higher education student and cultural capital. In fact the lack of exchange capital meant that the learning she had engaged in never obtained the status of cultural capital. Instead her learning became a form of wealth instead that she was unable to fully invest. In an economic sense wealth consists of savings that can be used for investments that in their turn create capital. Fanny did not have this possibility. The education capital she had was insufficient to create a significant cultural capital and the lack of exchangeable capital meant that she was unable to invest further in the education capital she had.

Our data and analyses here point to the importance of access to exchange capital in rural areas. Frans had access to this form of capital. Forest as private property enabled him and youngsters like him, with access to landed property or other forms of capital, to access opportunities that were beyond the reach of peers with more limited resources. And there was again great consistency in the data here. It can be seen in chapters two and three. Those who had more resources tended to express less criticism of the rural challenge (such as of distance). They also referred to concrete examples of the ways they could make use of the conversion of one capital form to another as a means to get on. They did not have to 'simply do their best and make do with what they had' (Fanny) and although they did not speak of social class relations as such in these circumstances, social class in terms of private ownership over the means of economic production was so obviously still a very significant feature in relation to who was able to do what, when and why with/in their education careers by influencing what kind of educational experiences and engagements were materially available, realistically considered and chosen. For the less *well-to-do*, the extended geographic distance in remote rural areas formed not only an inconvenience but also a serious mobility problem.

When considering this argument we might relate also to Lévi Strauss (1963) and Iris Marion Young's (2004) concept of structure and the reproduction of inequalities, which these authors suggest is primarily made by structural injustices not through individual creativity or ingenuity. They take place within legal frameworks of economic and cultural politics that have developed historically and in ways that have consistently enabled (and enable) some groups of people to have vastly more access to resources than others, both by having better tools for recognising and nurturing individual merit (SOU, 1990:44) and by having access to greater levels of power and influence to determine the terms of common life (ibid). When the official structures are weak alternatives are drawn and the terms of this struggle, as both historical and cultural geographic research suggest, are equally and neither both rural and urban at the same time. They are structural and class-related phenomena (Åberg-Bengtsson, 2009; Beach, 2018; Hayley, 2017).

Compensatory forms of capital in rural areas and schools

The division and regulation of property rights and ownership are identified as significantly important for education possibilities and access to other fluid forms of capital in the previous section. However, we are not trying to suggest these relations are determinate and systemic in the strictest sense. They are not. Indeed, education is regarded in modern state policy as a means of creating social prosperity, social cohesion, and economic growth, not as an institution within which these dimensions are reproduced and reflected only. These are of course the foundations of educational investment within human capital theory, which is the most influential economic theory of Western education and one that rural youngsters buy into, as suggested in chapter three. It has been setting the framework of government policies in Sweden for decades, where education investment has been identified as a key determinant of economic performance. However, at the same time national and international research still indicates that children from low socio-economic and ethnic households and communities develop academic skills slower than children from higher socio-economic and ethnic groups, regardless of other contextual factors of background such as urban or rural location (Yang Hansen and Gustafsson, 2018) and that childhood in low socio-economic and ethnic households is related to cognitive, language and memory development as well as socioemotional processing, and consequently also even poor income and health in adulthood.

Access to economic capital was important to educational access and what advantages were possible to make from educational opportunitis. But both students and teachers referred to other forms of capital as well as the importance of family ties and social relations (see chapter five) in rural areas of a kind similar to that discussed in Putnam and Gross (2002) concerning the concept of *bonding social capital*. Bonding social capital is formed from dense social networks and close relationships. On the positive side it helps cushion against social challenges, on the negative side it risks creating social closure and tends to be exclusionary. And both sides of this equation are found in the accounts of living and learning in rural regions as they are also in urban spaces too (Beach and Sernhede, 2011; Beach, 2018). It refers principally towards social organisations, norms and networks that are formed in relationships that can extend far back in time according to informants and tends to be strongest in local conditions where people are supposedly known and trusted by everyone in the locality.

Kinship and strong positive neighbourly relations emerged in the data and analysis in chapter five as an important factor in everyday life for forming bonding social capital, and in some cases also bridging social capital, through close contacts and relationships that were described by both students and teachers and that facilitated ways of handling the practicalities of everyday life (e.g. getting lifts to school or training sessions and summer jobs). These forms of capital were especially valuable for those with limited financial resources, where having a reliable older sibling, granddad, friend or neighbour was helpful in everyday life and for meeting the challenges of unexpected events. Emotional capital as a form of cultural capital that includes trans-situational feelings that are activated in people in specific social situations can supplement and even supplant these other capital forms under certain situations (Cottingham, 2016); which indeed as suggested in chapter five they actually also seemed to do in the case of the extreme situation of new arrivals in the currently hyper-diverse conditions created in the aftermath of mass war-, poverty- and hunger-diaspora. One of the teachers at Forest School, who had lived in the area for some time, expressed things as follows.

> People tend to try to solve most things themselves ... A lot of things have been closed down ... One tries to arrange things oneself instead as it is sometimes difficult to recruit people. (Forest School, May 23)

These points about the importance of structures of support for engaging in social actions like active education choice-making in rural areas have also been attended to in a recent article by Farrugia (2016).

Structures of support and the mobility imperative

That young people from rural areas can risk finding themselves losing the opportunity to make good on their investments in primary and secondary school learning when the opt to engage in upper-secondary studies unless they can exercise mobility is an obvious fact in Sweden and other countries with large remote rural areas. Moreover, this need is also escalating through the ever increasing concentration of economic and cultural capital in cities and the reduction of education access for rural populations (Fjellman et al., 2018). In the previous section capital mobility across three dimensions is important for enhanced mobility and it is these said possibilities to access an education in later years that helps young people to make good on their earlier learning investments. These dimensions are called the structural, the symbolic and the non-representational (Farrugia, 2011; Cottingham, 2016). They were related to but not wholly determined by material inequalities in resource ownership. Indeed resource ownership may affect resource access (to institutions) within local rural places to a greater degree than in urban areas as the mobility imperative may be becoming excessively extended (Haley, 2017).

Chapters 4 and 5 identify the importance of mobility quite distinctly as a social imperative for the students and adults who participated in our project, who seemed to regard moving to a city for educational reasons as inescapable. This is the material geographic aspect of mobility that accords with physical distance and physical access. The other forms of mobility are social and cultural. They sometimes coincide with the physical, such as occurs when *centrum*-periphery relationships of social inequality emerge in geographical space, but they are essentially qualitatively different forms of mobility and they are apparent even across short physical differences: such as across a city and even just sometimes a river, as described by for instance Lundberg in her thesis from 2015. In these circumstances, moving physically is not a crucial problem for students from urban areas, but territorial stigmatisation may be problematic and may cause both symbolic and social-psychological non-representational hindrances.

These challenges are identified in research. As is indicated there, a short move to another school is often undertaken on the new school markets by students and students from under-privileged areas, but mainly by the socio-economically more privileged individuals in these areas, with this thus adding further weight to existing segregations (Bunar and Ambrose, 2018; Forsberg, 2018). It shows then that there are differences between urban and rural areas in terms of how the mobility imperative is made effective and is undertaken. They exist in terms of the different mobility aspects that need to be overcome and the different forms of capital that will need to be created and used in order to fulfil the imperative of mobility under these different conditions. In urban areas the main mobility challenges are social and symbolic ones, with this creating concomitantly a need for the creation and use of social and symbolic forms of capital. In rural areas these requirements may exist for some individuals through *centrum*-periphery relationships, but on a far smaller scale that can be overcome through social familiarity in the rural spaces. A far greater challenge is physical mobility that is being accentuated through the uneven spatial materialisation of the quasi-market and the differentiated mobilities of upper secondary students (Fjellman, 2019). In line with Farrugia (2016) access to capital is more significant than just physical distance, as family circumstances either imposes additional constraints or offers support and solutions. As one teacher put things:

> Some families can give support (but) this year some of the parents of some of the year 9 students have told me that they can't provide the upper secondary school education their child want because they can't afford it.
> (Forest School, March 27)

These issues obviously concern how material conditions can impose harsh realities that limit education and for that matter also social, cultural and recreational possibilities and choices and subsequently the future prospects for young people not only (but perhaps particularly) in rural areas (Östhe et al.; Fjellman et al., 2018). This can be broken by access to economic and other forms of capital, which then also has effects on (and exacerbates) the already growing tendencies toward social reproduction in ways that run completely counter to the expressed ambitions of educational class parity from Sweden's folk-home welfare state and education project (SOU, 1948:27; Lgr 62, 69, 80; Lpo, 1994). Both families and local councils are trying, in different ways, to adapt to the situation of reduced possibilities and hardened economic climate. These conditions are in reality hard to resist and the principal adaptation of the youths from the countryside does, to a large degree, seem on the surface to be toward moving to a city with challenges for both the individuals and the society.

The final paragraph above might point at a dominant tendency that has been identified in the chapter with regard to the overall commitment expressed by students in rural secondary schools toward valuing education enough to be prepared to travel for it on the one hand, and toward them using the education they obtain as a lever to help them move away from their region of origin on a permanent basis on the other. That is, the paragraph speaks in the voice of a hegemonic tendency toward middle-class aspirationalism on the one hand and the vitality of urban lifestyle in the global economy on the other. However, this acquiescence to hegemonic discourse would not do the data and analyses presented in book justice if it was to be left completely unattended to and unchallenged. There were other discourses and there was resistance. Counter urban discourses have to be mentioned here and there were examples of intentions from individuals to use education as tool to help one stay in an area or return to it after acquiring valuable skills and knowledge outside. Education was not only talked about in rural areas as a vehicle of escape! Sometimes quite the opposite was stated and there are also of course; though we registered few of them in our collected data; instances where some students expressed complete ambiguity toward education and the role of education in fashioning future identities and life chances.

Areas that are feared, derided or just inadequately comprehended by the dominant class may not be experienced in the same way by all (Beach, 2017). Education understood and acted towards as a means for the exercise of middle-class aspiration and a tool for escaping from places and their social relations is an aspect of dominant class hegemony. It is, as hegemony always is, challenged and fought over in everyday life, and there are countless examples of transcendence of this dominant hegemony in the empirical data. The examples in chapter five stand out, but they are found across all chapters.

Discussion

Relationships between people and education change when the material histories of the areas they are in change. They do so also with some local and unique characteristics, but these are formed in (and will reflect) certain patterns of consistency and continuity. One of them is the issue of social class. Although rarely specifically voiced as such by research subjects in the investigations, the social class dimension in the development of individual relationships to, possibilities in and chances taken concerning education is quite emphatic, as what we have discerned is that despite other differences, social class background was ultimately a decisive factor for what became of education at the individual level across the sites. This applied moreover irrespective of the characteristics of place, such as semi-, emergent-, stable-, or de-industrialising urbanisation area (on the one hand), or remote rural or sparsely populated area on the other.

Several factors coupled to the impact of capital flows in the different rural areas have signified this importance of social class, with the possibilities created by private ownership of (and control over) swathes of *natural capital* being the most obvious one at the individual level. However, geological and bio-topic capital and levels of accessibility tended to determine levels of capitalist interest and degrees of first semi-, then intensive and finally also (after exhaustion) even de-industrialisation, with this in its turn creating massively changed population concentrations, the introduction of vertical and horizontal divisions of labour and the need of *in situ* social institutions. The presence of identified and accessible natural capital and the creation of a local labour force enabled an entirely new local social structure compared to that of the past. Particular mechanisms were involved. A class structure was grounded and forms of class reproduction were identifiable in relation to education processes and outcomes that are still visible.

In the industrialised rural towns coming from a working class background tended (but did not always) accord with a notion of the factory (or the mine) as being good enough for me, my neighbours and my family before me with this then working in favour of keeping a person in place. But in sparsely populated and more remote or *original* rural areas the holding discourse (in terms of keeping economically weaker individuals back) was differently constructed and more directly coupled to issues of property on the one hand and a positive local discourse about things like the freedom, challenge and beauty of nature on the other (as again expressed by Fanny). These are outcomes that suggest that Massey's question (1984) concerning whether what are considered as only regional problems realy are only regional can be answered with a loud and clear "No". Instead, what seem to be local and specific problems have origins in particular historical class formations but must also be understood in relation to a more general history and traditions of law, order, and hegemony that link them also to events in other places as well. It involves recognising how schools are implicated as institutional apparatuses in the politics of social and cultural change (transformation) on the one hand and conservation on the other, but where social reproduction tends to prevail through more (and richer) education possibilities befalling those who need them least and less, compared to those who, from the perspective of social equity and distributive justice, need and deserve them more (Beach, 2018).

These effects of hegemony and structural inequality are visible in the present book and can be seen in patterns of education access and *use* both within rural areas and between them, as well as between rural areas in general and urban ones, in general: i.e. they are both and neither rural, urban and sub-urban phenomena at one and the same time. They are instead capitalist distinctions that appear in and through different local patterns of behavior, talk and interaction in education spaces (chapters two and three) and they signal a serious systemic need to strengthen and deepen democracy not just in rural areas but for and in the interests of people in these areas and beyond. The global development of urbanisation and the prevalence of metro-centricity are not established haphazardly and they benefit an extractionist urban oligarchy that returns little of value to either rural or urban areas (Beach, 2018). For as pointed out by Lefebvre (2000), the politics of spatial economic exploitation are not confined to the city, as the relationship of center and periphery is evidenced also in developing countries and in rural and other marginal regions of capitalist countries through causal efficacies in the forces and relations of production in rural as well as in urban areas.

These are points that have also been made by Lefebvre (2000) relating to the ways in which mobile (corporate and manufacturing) capital has been created and grown in importance in rural areas in terms of the divisions it creates through extraction colonisation and the technification of production, to first supplant feudal property relations and the forms of tribal capital (property) that had preceded it by the land and vagrancy acts. In this way, and supported by political Law, property has lost any semblance of a communal institution and today even the modern State has fallen into the hands of the private owners of mobile capital through the commercial credit which the owners of capital, the bourgeois, control.

The bourgeoisie has evolved from a class within the nation state to an entity that exists both beside and outside of civil society. Indeed the bourgeoisie now has extensive control over the State, which now exists primarily for the sake of legislating in the interests (and protection of the rights) of private property. Even in and around rural areas and its forms of natural, mobile and settled capital, and where members of the bourgeoisie are less notably physically present, the presence of the interests of capital are still as visible, with this representing the obvious continuity in terms of power struggles and their manifestations in rural and global areas that also becomes apparent and manifest even in terms of educational presence, availability and patterns of educational use. Social reproduction is a clear fact in relation to rural education processes, availabilities, outcomes, experiences and anticipations: Economic distributions match class divisions, and the best (and most) educational opportunities go to and are expected and availed of by those who need them least in order to advance and live a good life. Moreover, even history exhibits the negation of the state role in a positive sense of the transformation of class power structures, by operating instead in terms of the refinement of the instruments and institutions of reproduction comprised by local schools that so very clearly, in both urban and rural areas, work in the interests of the dominant class.

References

Åberg-Bengtsson, L. (2009). The smaller the better? A review of research on small rural school in Sweden, *International Journal of Educational Research*, 48(2): 100-109.

Beach, D. (2018). *Structural injustices in Swedish Education.* Singapore: Palgrave MacMillan.

Beach, D. (2017). Whose justice is this! Capitalism, class and education justice and inclusion in the Nordic countries: race, space and class history, *Education Review*, 69(5): 620-637.

Beach, D., From, T., Johansson, M. and Öhrn, E. (2018). Educational and spatial justice in rural and urban areas in three Nordic countries: A meta-ethnographic analysis. *Education Inquiry*, 9(1) 4-21.

Beach, D., Johansson, M., Rosvall, P-Å., Rönnlund, M and Öhrn, E. (2018). Rurality and education relations: Metro-centricity and local values in rural communities and rural schools. *European Educational Research Journal*, 18(1): 19-33.

Beach, D. and Sernhede, O. 2011. From Learning to Labour to Learning for Marginality: School Segregation and Marginalisation in Swedish Suburbs, *British Journal of Sociology of Education* 32(2): 257-274.

Bunar, N. and Ambrose, A. (2016). Schools, choice and reputation: Local school markets and the distribution of symbolic capital in segregated cities. *Research in Comparative and International Education*, Vol.11(1): 34-51.

Corbett, M., (2015a). Towards a rural sociological imagination: ethnography and schooling in mobile modernity. *Ethnography and Education* 10: 263-277.

Corbett, M. (2015b). Rural education: some sociological provocations for the field. *Australian and International Journal of Rural Education*, 25(3): 9.

Cottingham, M. D. (2016). Theorizing emotional capital, Theory and Society, 45(5): 451-470.

Farrugia, D. (2016.) The mobility imperative for rural youth: the structural, symbolic and non-representational dimensions rural youth mobilities, *Journal of Youth Studies*, 19(6): 836-851.

Fjellman, A-M. (2019). *School choice, space and the geography of marketization : analyses of educational restructuring in upper secondary education in Sweden.* Diss. (summary) Göteborg : University of Gothenburg.

Fjellman, A-M., Yang Hansen, K. and Beach, D. (2018). School choice and implications for equity: the new political geography of the Swedish upper secondary school market. *Educational Review*, 71(4):518-53.

Forsberg, H. (2018). Gymnasieval och segregation, in Fejes, A. and Dahlstedt, M., (Eds.) *Skolan, Marknaden och framtiden.* Lund: Studentlitteratur.

Haley, A. (2017). *Geographical Mobility of the Tertiary Educated—Perspectives from Education and Social Space.* (Diss.). Göteborgs universitet. Utbildningsvetenskapliga fakulteten. University of Gothenburg: Faculty of Education

Johansson, M (2017) 'Yes, the power is in the town': An ethnographic study of student participation in a rural Swedish secondary school. *Australian and International Journal of Rural Education* 27(2): 61-76.

Lefebvre, H. (2000/1974). *La production de l'espace*, 4e edition. Paris: Anthropos.

Lévi-Strauss, C. (1963). *Structural Anthropology*, trans. Claire Jacobson and Brooke Grundfest Schoepf, New York: Basic Books.

Lgr 62, Lgr 69, Lgr 80: National curriculum for the compulsory comprehensive school 1962, 1969, 1980. Stockholm: National Superior School Board.

Lpo 1994: National curriculum for the compulsory comprehensive school 1994. Stockholm: National Schools Agency.

Maisuria, A. (2016). Obscured Inequality and Feasible Equity: An Exploratory Study of Life History, Consciousness and Practices of Social Class in Sweden. PhD. University College London, Institute of Education. Unpublished PhD thesis.

Massey, D. (1994). *Space, place and gender*. Cambridge: Polity Press.

OECD 2005. *Equity in Education Thematic Review:* Sweden. www.oecd.org/sweden/38697408.pdf

Östh, J., Andersson,E., and Malmberg,B., 2013. School choice and increasing performance difference: A counter factual approach, *Urban Studies*, 50(2) 407-425. https://doi.org/10.1177/0042098012452322

Putnam, R. and Gross, K. (2002*). Democracies in Flux: The Evolution of Social Capital in Contemporary Society.* Oxford: Oxford University Press.

Richardson, G. 2010. *Svensk ubtbildningshistoria: skola och samhälle förr och nu.* [Swedish education history: Schools and society then and now] Lund: Studentlitteratur.

SOU 1948: 27. *Skolkommissionens betänkande med förslag till riktlinjer för det Svenska skolväsendets utveckling* [The Deliberations of the National School Commission Concerning Guidelines for the Development of the Swedish School System]. Stockholm: Ecklesiastikdepartementet.

SOU 1990:44. *Demokrati och makt i Sverige: Maktutredningens huvudrapport. [Power and democracy in Sweden: The Final Report of the Power and Democracy Commission]* Statens offentliga utredningar. *Stockholm.*

SOU 2017:35. Samling för skolan: nationell strategi för kunskap och likvärdighet : slutbetänkande 2015 års Skolkommision. [Gathering for school: National strategy for knowledge and equivalence] Stockholm : Wolters Kluwer.

SOU (2017). *För Sveriges landsbygder—en sammanhållen politik för arbete, hållbar tillväxt och välfärd.* [For the Swedish countryside—a coherent politic for work, sustainability and welfare] SOU 2017: 1 and 2. Näringslivsdepartementet.

Stenbacka, J. (2011). Othering the rural: About the construction of rural masculinities and the unspoken urban hegemonic ideal in Swedish media. *Journal of Rural Studies.* Volume 27, Issue 3, pp. 235-244.

Swedish Government Proposition 1991/92:95. Om valfrihet och fristående skolor. Stockholm: Regeringen.

Verger, A. Fontdevila, C., Zancajo, A. and Steiner-Khamsi, G. (2016). *Privatization of education: a political economy of global education reform* (International perspectives on educational reform series). Columbia, New York: Teachers College Press.

Yang Hansen, K. and Gustavsson, J-E. (2018). Changes in the impact of family education on student educational achievement in Sweden 1988-2014. *Scandinavian journal of educational research*, Vol. 62(5): 719-736.

Young, I. M. (2004). "Five Faces of Oppression", in Maree Heldke, Lisa; O'Conor, Peg. *Oppression, Privilege, and Resistance: Theoretical Perspectives on Racism, Sexism, and Heterosexism.* McGraw-Hill.pp. 37-63.

Chapter 8

Closing discussion

Dennis Beach and Elisabet Öhrn

Introduction

Collectively the chapters in this book provide insights into several neglected aspects of education in rural spaces. First, they show that relevant conditions in rural areas are much less homogenous than often implied in metrocentric research. However, despite the variations there are consistent patterns of continued social and educational inequities between rural and urban areas. Previous research has shown that cities have grown and developed, whilst almost half of the country's rural municipalities have smaller populations today than three decades ago (Fjellman, Yang Hansen and Beach, 2018). Moreover, partly due to changes driven by the increasing marketisation of education, schools are closing in rural areas and students have to travel more often, for longer times and distances (at greater costs with less state subsidy) to obtain their education than before (Fjellman et al., 2018). Thus, in terms of access to educational resources, students from rural areas are disadvantaged. The analyses described in the previous chapters detected two main responses by students and teachers in the rural areas to their inferior position in relation to peers in urban settings. Some seemed to accept it, and tried to mitigate its adverse consequences, while others criticised the metrocentricity, current denial of their rural material and social hardships, and neglect of their assets.

Spatial consistencies in Sweden have also been noted in the recent National School Commission report (SOU, 2017), together with differences related to family income, parental occupation and parental education. According to the report, these differences are wider in rural than in urban spaces, and linked to factors such as social class and levels of integration in the global economy. Moreover, the differences between rural and urban areas increase on average at each consecutive stage of the education system. It also notes that poor educational outcomes are typically concentrated in areas where other forms of disadvantage are centred. Consequently, there are some schools with high levels of disadvantage. In such cases, rather than offering a route to social mobility and equality, the education system reproduces inequality and future life difficulties, particularly for learners with little access to the forms of social and cultural capital favoured by the system.

Key highlighted results

We believe that several features of results presented in the empirical chapters warrant particular attention, and thus are discussed below in relation to two broad themes. The first, *Youths' images of places and spatial conditions*, concerns the places and the second, *School presentations of places and values*, concerns experiences of schools within them.

Youths' images of places and spatial characteristics and groups

According to our theoretical framework, rooted in concepts formulated by Massey (1994/2013) different social groups and individuals have distinct positions in relation to ebbs and flows in the evolving global capitalist political economy of signs, privileges, materials and possibilities as spatial distinctions strongly influence the development of identity, senses of well-being, and levels and types of social integration. In addition, the interconnections between different forms of capital in different spaces influence, but do not determine, positions, experiences and power in relation to the flows, and movement. They represent *social relations* corresponding to a definite stage of production that can also be seen historically, in Marxist terms, as the division of labour leads initially to the separation of industrial and commercial from agricultural labour, and hence the separation of town and country, and conflicts of interests between them. Then comes a separation of commercial from industrial labour as expressions of different forms of property, where the division of labour also determines individuals' relations to one another (Marx and Engels, 1932). In the present context, the local rural places' historical (capital) relations shape the conditions of production for youth identities, possibilities, future prospects and relationships.

The empirical findings presented in the other chapters confirm that different social groups and places have distinct relationships to differentiated forms of mobility, and the influential factors include educational availabilities. *Inter alia*, groups' and individuals' abilities to initiate and respond to flows and movements of goods, capital and resources vary massively. For example, children of refugees and undocumented migrant workers often have few possibilities to exert influence over their situation, and can experience alienation (see chapter five).

Youth identities, possibilities and future lives

An important factor influencing the relations and changes explored in the empirical chapters is the evolution of (formerly national and now global) industrial capitalism. The penetration of capitalist production, and the forms it took in different regions (and in relation to other aspects of human sociality and nature), triggered massive reorganisations of vast areas of rural Sweden, with pockets of semi- and peri-urban industrialisation and settlement in some places, whilst other areas were left relatively untouched. Centrifugal and centripetal effects on rural areas varied substantially following this: populations and resources were pushed out of some areas and drawn into others.

In terms of phenomena discussed in the empirical chapters, education relations in local communities are partly shaped by these developments in relations to the conditions of economic and cultural production. As Marx and Engels (1932) commented, private property alienates the individuality of both people and things. Landowners can lease or sell their lands without the land itself losing any of its inherent features initially and the subsequent feature of change reflects the extent and existence of the social relations that are created and destroyed, which occurs without the further assistance of individual landed proprietors. Landowners exerted control over the conditions of material life and subsequently the relationships educational institutions formed to the places they were housed in too, and the different social classes of inhabitants there too (chapter six).

In its undeveloped form private property is the simple relation of the individual to the natural world in which their individuality finds objective expression, but under capitalism the possession of private property took the form of the right of an individual to exclude others from the use of an object, in this case land and what was on or under it, and created the conditions for the rupture of society into classes. Private property for some became essentially the denial of the private property of others and it subsequently found its ultimate expression in relation to the imperative of wage-labour for the materially dispossessed. These class relations and their history have never been discussed in schools in rural areas in the project according to the empirical chapters. And yet they are fundamental to its present characteristics and also to the ways educational opportunities have developed, become recognised and have then been availed of by rural individuals historically and at present.

The analyses in the different chapters have revealed major differences within and among the local areas, in students' reflections on their education future and work, and show that they took structural relations of the local labour market into consideration. For instance, in places mainly offering unskilled manual and service work there was a stronger tendency to aim for upper secondary programmes oriented towards such work than in areas with a more varied labour market and more highly educated population (chapter four). Overall chances of future work in the places were also considered when discussing future options of staying or returning. The young people often spoke in appreciative terms of their present residential area and expressed a desire to stay there or return, although some considered it unlikely given the local labour market. Thus, their considerations appear to support the conclusion of Brox (2006, p. 47) that the centrality of economic organisation is a key factor for the maintenance of local communities.

The *leaving or staying* issue, which is so central in much rural research literature (Waara, 2011), was also a core concern of these young people. It related to the same sets on injunctions of education and labour property as those discussed above and was expressed most clearly when they were asked to reflect on their future. Differences were again found among the students in the six municipalities. For students living in municipalities with a school offering a wide range of upper secondary education programmes, or within commuting distance of such a school, decisions about staying or leaving could wait until after they had finished upper secondary school. However, students living in other municipalities had to address the issue more urgently, as daily commuting was only possible if they chose one of the potentially limited programmes offered by the closest upper secondary school. Other choices would require weekly commuting, or a permanent move close to a school in another area (chapter four).

Labour market relations, as manifested in parents' occupations and class positions, were also important for youth's understandings of work and how they visualised their own futures. However, the young people themselves rarely referred to social relations, controversies or divergence in terms of social class or strata, or economic differences (as shown, for example, in chapter six), and did not seem to view such categorisations as determining or structural factors (chapter two). In this respect, urban youth appear more inclined to discuss relations explicitly in terms of social class, and refer to differences in people's income, education and migrant background as major elements of their social positioning (e.g. Öhrn, 2011). Indeed it has been suggested that one reason that class (and migrancy) might stand out as less central categorisations in rural areas is that it is not made visible in distinct segregated housing and schooling similar to urban areas (Öhrn, 2012a), where the social differences and contractions are more visibly evident (cf. Sernhede, 2007).

However, the conception of *place* as a signifier of certain social and material relations appeared to be as central in the rural schools as in previously researched urban ones (cf. Öhrn and Weiner, 2007). But whereas in urban research place is typically found to be distinctly classed and ethnified (e.g. Arnesen, 2002; Beach and Sernhede, 2011; Gitz-Johansen, 2003), in rural schools it seemed at first glance rather to be underpinned by notions of *centrum* and periphery; between those living in the central village/town where the school was located and those outside of it, and was mirrored in students' as well as teachers' descriptions of various groupings.

The importance of place and spatial conditions was also manifested in students' interactions. Those who lived outside the central village/town travelled to school together by bus and arrived (together) at school earlier, then left later, than those who lived within walking distance of the school. However, there were indications of class underpinnings in these arrangements in some comments by teachers, as living in or outside the villages was seen as related to parents' educational capital and attitudes towards studies (chapter six). Thus, although understandings of class appear less salient in the researched rural schools than in urban ones, further exploration of its manifestations and significance may be required, particularly for the young people in de/industrialised villages/towns. This is corroborated by the importance of material resources, raised especially by students in interviews, with references to the injustices of rural life, the importance of Nature for rural livelihoods and their financial considerations in relation to future education and work prospects.

Structural injustice and urban-rural relationships

The phenomena observed and discussed above are clearly consistent with the theoretical concepts about place and space developed by Massey (1994/2013), and previous conceptualisations by Marx and Engels (1932). Yet as stated earlier, and noted by Bourdieu and Passeron (1970), identity is as much a structural phenomenon that individuals become embroiled in (Nylund, 2012) as it is a phenomenon that is principally of individual making, although it is of course influenced by individual actions, values and appreciation as well.

The concept of structural oppression formulated by Lévi Strauss (1963) and Young (2004) is also relevant to our considerations of rural educational spaces, rural places and youths' identities and experiences. According to these authors, the reproduction of inequalities is driven by structural injustices rather than individual's capacities (Young, 2001, 2004). This is held to occur through the (symbolic) violence and harm (reproduction of violently disruptive capitalist ideology and practices) resulting from legal, political, economic and cultural rules, regulations and norms (Beach, Johansson, Öhrn, Rönnlund and Rosvall, 2018). The arenas of such symbolic violence are institutions like schools (Cole, 2003) that have developed historically in ways that enable some people to have more access to resources than others.

This inequality of enablement involves some people having better tools for acquiring resources and nurturing individual merit than others (Bernstein, 1971), and access to greater levels of power and influence to determine the terms of communication and assessment in common institutional life (Beach, 2018). The institutional arrangements involved include abstract economic, philosophical, social and psychological theories and practices, tax laws, international trade agreements, international, business and domestic law and school buildings, forms of communication, ideologies and curricula (Bernstein, 1971, 1975, 1990; Massey, 1994; Cole, 2003; Apple, 2004). They denote a confluence of institutional rules, physical structures and interactive routines such as those discussed in the preceding chapters, within a mobilisation of resources and historical givens in relation to which individuals have to act. They form deep social mechanisms that generate the socio-cultural forms that are lived in empirical reality and often emerge as alienating, exploitative forces (Apple, 2004; Maisuria and Beach, 2017; Beach, 2018). Originating from the modes of capitalist production and their inherent inequalities, they often hinder empowerment by reproducing patterns of unfairness, which may often seem to occur through consent to the status quo (Gramsci, 1971) but is still symbolically violent and potentially destabilising.

Structure, particularly concepts of the structure of class relations, have been quintessentially important when we have collectively interpreted our data concerning youths' experiences, educational possibilities and life chances. We define structure in line with Massey (1994/2013) and Young (2003), as the confluence of institutional relations whose collective consequences may not always bear the mark of any person or group's direct and knowing intention but have distinctly patterned social outcomes. Young was concerned here with large scale or macro structures and Massey with their penetration of and interpellations within particular places and spaces. Considering structure in these terms is necessary because as both of these authors have pointed out, our economic circumstances at birth are not equal, and people have to confront their local and specific life challenges with unique sets of options. Local conditions always constrain some people while enabling others. More strictly, they impose different constraints and enable different opportunities, because (for example) children of the very rich or very powerful may require constant guarding. This needs to be factored into any account of large-scale systemic outcomes of the operations of social institutions.

As shown throughout the previous chapters, the central *us* and *them* social relation expressed by youth in the researched areas was between those living in urban and rural areas. This was sometimes transposed by *centrum*-periphery distanciation perspectives, but in all the researched areas, rural living was described in relation to two urban discourses. One was about urban failure to understand nature (including its romanticisation) or cope with it, together with a critique of political metrocentricity and the lack of understanding of rural conditions. This was recorded mainly in the sparsely populated areas. The other discourse included negative imagery and pre-associations of rural places and spaces, denying the inherent value of active rurality and accepting the centrality of urbanities and wider world. In this discourse, the rural was not expressed as equally or substantially contributing to an interrelation but as benefitting from it.

School presentations of places and values

Urban education research has often highlighted the failure of schools to help youth in marginalised areas to understand their positions through teaching (e.g. Beach and Sernhede, 2011). Young people living in such areas are found to be aware of the *pathologising discourses* of their neighbourhoods (Archer, Hollingworth and Mendick, 2010, p. 32), but not how to address them. This is not to say that they dislike their schools—actually they often talk approvingly about their schools and teachers—but they are aware of their representations as problematic.

School content, rural positioning and valorisation

The analyses showed that students generally approved of their local context and schooling, as found in marginalised urban settings (cf. Öhrn, 2012b; Schwartz, 2013). However, the strength of their approval depended on whether (and if so how) the local context was represented in teaching, and substantially varied *between* the rural areas. As previously concluded (Beach, Johansson, Öhrn, Rönnlund and Rosvall, 2018), teachers in the de/industrial areas tended to accept and reproduce aspects of a dominant urban discourse that emphasises the importance of global interrelations and represents rural (and marginalised urban) areas as needy problematic contexts. This discourse was often accompanied by encouragement from agents of the schools for students to leave the area in order to obtain a better educational future and life opportunities. In contrast, in the sparsely populated areas, individuals described (and showed in school practices) an understanding of their area as useful in teaching and valuable both locally and nationally.

In other words, school practices in the de/industrialised villages tended to implicitly accept their dependency, the importance of social and global economic bonds, and hence the strong centrifugal forces pushing people and resources away. However, teachers and students in the sparsely populated areas did not accept this discourse so readily, positioning themselves more distinctly in the local context through the selection of curricular content. Furthermore, this was done in appreciative terms that emphasised the importance of rural resources for both those living there and the nation as a whole. This discourse was also repeatedly raised and heard in school interactions, local school interiors and the local curriculum, and—as pointed out above—in youth interviews (cf. Vigo and Soriano, 2014).

Frequently a major feature of this discourse was a strong emphasis on Nature, in terms of its value in material, recreational and survival terms as well as the characteristics of natural environments and ways of life. Such descriptions are well known from other rural contexts (e.g. Neal, 2002). However, as shown in chapter two, this was not done by drawing on a construction of a rural idyll, in contrast to recorded discourses in some other studies (e.g. Leyshon, 2008). Rather, idyllisation of nature was presented as part of a critique of urban people's estrangement from nature and failure to understand and cope with it. Indeed, rather than reproducing the concept of a rural idyll, economic conditions were described as harder than in other areas and decisions by politicians from outside the region were described as being dislocated from local consciousness and as making local life-style and survival even more problematic.

Historic voices and silences

Local histories and contemporary relations were addressed in the rural schools in a way seldom found in studies of urban schools. However, there seemed to be distinctly gender privileging forms of representation in place and some local (historic) themes and events were more likely to be addressed than others, with significant silences about some current or historic local conflicts.

In this respect our empirical data and analyses align with previous research noting that teachers tend to omit local conflicts from pedagogic content and tend to downplay the historical significance of women's labour power. For example, a well-known national historical landmark event that had major implications for the workers' movement and political struggle against capitalist exploitation occurred about fifty kilometres away from one of the schools, but it was not even mentioned in lessons covering the period (chapter three). Furthermore, when local history and culture were addressed in the rural schools, middle and upper class people, like doctors and foundry proprietors (usually men) were mentioned by name far more often than workers and indigenous people and male occupations were discoursed more often and more positively than women's (chapter six).

Consequently, there were silences similar to those in urban schools (e.g. Schwartz, 2013) about social controversies, conflicts, class relations and history. And accordingly, there also were certain elements of romanticising the history of, for instance, timber raftsmen. The history of indigenous people in the areas also tended to be romanticised, or silenced, which is rather startling, considering the closeness to Sámi areas and presence of students with Sámi backgrounds in some of the schools.

The current refugee situation in Sweden provides further examples of reluctance to address conflict. There were some expressions of conflicts, advantages and solidarity following the reception of refugees (chapter five). However, there were also some important silences, where challenges for the schools or communities were not mentioned although they appeared important from recorded conversations and processes in the individual schools. Staff and students sometimes discussed both the global and local migrant situations, but made no comment about, only briefly mentioned or even denied the presence of associated local problems (competing interests and lack of space, staff and funding). Teachers sometimes addressed such issues, but as pointed out in earlier chapters, they were often played down or ignored. Our analyses indicate that this might, at least sometimes, have been related to worries about playing into the hands of extreme right political forces, and fuelling nationalist or racist interpretations by mentioning difficulties associated with the refugee influx. However, as pointed out elsewhere (e.g. Gaine, 2005; Rosvall and Öhrn, 2014) it is not unusual for racism and xenophobia to be ignored by teachers. Taken together then, the contextualisations in local history and relations that have been made in the rural schools described in the project may have furthered some awareness of specific issues related to social justice in rural areas (e.g. metrocentrism), but they are unlikely to have fostered a broader understanding of the relations of power that currently structure the disfiguring of history and the misrepresentation of democratic political relationships.

Education politics and policies

Cities in Sweden's post-welfare society are distinctly segregated in terms of wealth, levels of higher education and ethnicity, with increasing economic exclusion in some regions. This is also the case in rural areas. However, rural areas are shrinking in population terms while cities are growing. Schools are closing, and particularly at upper secondary levels students are experiencing far greater difficulties in obtaining their rightful range of educational choices than previous rural students and peers in contemporary city areas (Fjellman et al., 2018).

However, accessibility is not the only determinant of educational justice and equality. They are also influenced by history, structural relations, political decisions, attitudes. Other important factors include the availability of appropriate pedagogy and a curriculum that builds on the experiences and understandings of all young people, across diversities, with full recognition and without marginalisation is also important. This is crucial for the provision of full agency and possibilities for students to develop and engage in their learning as fully as possible, regardless of who they are or where they are from (Raffo, 2011; Beach, 2018). Our research clearly suggests that although they may not always recognise or express significant dissatisfaction, the children of the rural spaces are not favoured by the currently predominant metrocentrism. This implies a need to research the ways in which the particular concerns of groups or individuals are first negotiated in relation to education decisions, by whom, by what rights and constitutions, and under what socially understood and obvert conditions, before being written into formal policy.

These are matters of educational politics and policy, but there is more at stake. The pedagogic content and experiences, as well as developed concepts of self-as-learner and conceptions of future education, provide grounds to question the ideas of educational justice and equity expressed in manifestoes of a series of centre-left and centre-right elected governments. Educational justice and equity are still formal aims of the education system even under market governance (Lundahl, Erixon Arreman, Holm and Lundström, 2013, 2014).

Thus, education should still be socially just and equitable at all levels, regardless of gender, ethnic, religious, geographical and socioeconomic background. This is now supposed to be delivered via competition between schools and the exercise of personal responsibility and freedom of choice, with parity between rural and urban areas and spaces within them. However, as this book clearly shows, there is no such parity. Moreover, there are disparities in terms of rural and urban space related to social class, gender, race/ethnicity, place of domicile (Fjellman et al., 2018), and other dimensions not addressed in this study, such as sexuality and disability (Vaahtera, Niemi, Lappalainen and Beach, 2017).

These are also features of rural-urban inequality and structural injustice. Moreover, they have been exacerbated by transmogrification of the notion of a comprehensive *education for all* into the ability to exercise personal choice, based on the individualisation of rights and promotion of dominant economic and private interests (Berhanu, 2016). As the empirical chapters suggest, educational opportunities in relation to aspects of urban and rural space are highly political and ideologically biased in favour of urbanism, while educational opportunities within rural spaces still distinctly socially and culturally reproductive. *Plus ça change, plus c'est la même chose.* But this could not be clearer than in relation to the exercise of the new arbiter of justice and equality in education following market reforms in the education system: i.e. the principal of personal choice.

Choices are not available in the same way in rural areas as in urban ones and often rural youths will have to travel significant distances to obtain their upper-secondary schooling. Rural choice is really, as discussed in chapter four, a choice of to travel or not travel. It is a question of *travel and make good* or *stay and make do* quite simply, and the possession of valuable forms of capital; sometimes social but mainly though economic capital in this case; becomes the key arbiter of social injustice and access in these circumstances. Indeed this is one way in which structural injustice works. Economic capital not only breaks down distances for the children of the rich, the absence of economic capital makes distances insurmountable for the children of poor. Economic capital renders distance into a resource for the rich in the exclusion of the children of the poor from the prestigious and desirable educational choices they want for their own children. Situations are overdetermined but at the last instance the bell of economic determinism does still seem to be the one that tolls loudest in relation to educational and life possibilities even in rural (and thus not just) in urban areas. It is significant in many ways from national politics of scale and urban agglomeration to institutional bias and social distinctions all the way down to individual choice possibilities and their socio-cultural socio-economic mechanisms.

There is a history involved here. Productive capital in rural areas in Sweden has historically been associated with agriculture, forestry, mining, and manufacture of timber and wood-pulp. We have shown that while these productive forces remain important in given rural areas, spatial vitality seems to be identified in terms of the local production economy and its position within a global network of capitalistic relations, which are also reflected in educational curriculum selections and interactions (Beach, Johansson, Öhrn, Rönnlund and Rosvall, 2018). However, when agricultural, mining, or production industries are not present, other foundations of spatial value are used to express an understanding of local places as being vital social and cultural spaces and other features of social class determination of educational worth and possibilities take over (ibid). Social class, and by all means as identified in for instance chapter six gender too, are significant shapers of educational content, curriculum interactions and educational possibilities in schools in all rural areas, with interesting variations relating to area type and spatial characteristics and history.

Concluding remarks

In this book, we have identified various features of such understanding in terms of curriculum interactions, forms of representation and the classification and framing of educational content. They challenge ideas of rurality as being typified by isolation, poverty, marginalisation, depopulation, conservatism, racism, exclusion and, particularly, passivity and the negative valuations of rurality as semi-fictional hegemonic products of modernity and postmodernity that are ideologically imposed on rural spaces (Bagley and Hillyard, 2014). Our findings indicate that local people both transcend hegemony and construct a positive concept of the value of rural spaces and carve out a meaningful place for education in relation to these local value sets, while still contributing to social reproduction in and through educational interactions.

References

Apple, M. W., (2004) *Ideology and curriculum,* 25th anniversary 3rd edition, New York: Routledge.

Archer, l., Hollingworth, S. and Mendick, H., (2010) *Urban youth and schooling: the experiences and identities of educationally 'at risk' young people*, Maidenhead: Open University Press.

Arnesen, A-L., (2002) *Ulikhet og marginalisering. Med referanse til kjønn og sosial bakgrunn. En etnografisk studie av sosial og diskursiv praksis i skolen.* [Difference and marginality in relation to gender and social background. An ethnographic study of social and discursive praxis at school], Thesis, Oslo, Norway: University of Oslo, Unipub Forlag.

Bagley, C. and Hillyard, S., (2014) Rural schools, social capital and the Big society, *British Educational Research Journal,* 40(1): 63-78.

Beach, D., (2018) *Structural Injustices in Swedish Education,* Singapore: Palgrave MacMillan.

Beach, D., Johansson, M., Öhrn, E., Rönnlund, M. and Rosvall, P-Å., (2018) Rurality and education relations: Metro-centricity and local values in rural communities and rural schools, *European Educational Research Journal,* https://doi.org/10.1177/1474904118780420

Beach, D. and Sernhede, O., (2011) From learning to labour to learning for marginality: school segregation and marginalisation in Swedish suburbs, *British Journal of Sociology of Education,* 32(2): 257-274.

Berhanu, G., (2016) Contemporary Swedish society and education: inequities and challenges, in D. Beach and A. Dyson (eds.), *Equity and education in cold climates,* London: Tufnell Press.

Bernstein, B., (1971) *Class, Codes and Control: Volume 1—Theoretical Studies Towards A Sociology of Language,* London: Routledge.

Bernstein, B., (1975) *Class, codes and control: Volume 3—towards a theory of educational transmissions* (1977 2nd ed.), London: Routledge.

Bernstein, B., (1990) *Class, codes and control, vol. 4: The structuring of pedagogic discourse,* London: Routledge.

Bourdieu, P. and Passeron, J. C., (1970/1977) *Reproduction in education, society and culture,* London: Sage.

Brox, O., (2006) *The political economy of rural development,* Delft: Eburon Academic Publishers.

Cole, M., (2003) Might it be in the practice that it fails to succeed? A Marxist critique of claims for postmodernism and poststructuralism as forces for social change and social justice, *British Journal of Sociology of Education,* 24(4): 487-500.

Fjellman, A-M., Yang Hansen, K. and Beach, D., (2018) School choice and implications for equity: the new political geography of the Swedish upper secondary school market, *Educational Review,* DOI: 10.1080/00131911.2018.1457009

Gaine, C., (2005) *We're all different, thanks: the persisting myth about white schools,* Stoke on Trent: Trentham.

Gitz-Johansen, T., (2003) Representations of ethnicity: How teachers speak about ethnic minority students, in D. Beach, T. Gordon and E. Lahelma (eds.), *Democratic education. Ethnographic challenges* (pp. 66-79), London: The Tufnell Press.

Gramsci, A., (1971) *Selections from the Prison Notebooks,* Free download: https://qbh05crfw06.storage.googleapis.com/MDcxNzgwMzk3WA==06.pdf

Lévi Strauss, C., (1963) *Structural Anthropology,* (trans. Claire Jacobson and Brooke Grundfest Schoepf), New York: Basic Books.

Leyshon, M., (2008) The betweeness of being a rural youth: inclusive and exclusive lifestyles, *Social and Cultural Geography,* 9(1): 1-26.

Lundahl, L., Erixon Arreman, I., Holm, A. and Lundström, U., (2013) Educational marketization the Swedish way, *Education Inquiry,* 4(3): 497-517.

Lundahl, L., Erixon Arreman, I., Holm, A-S. and Lundström, U., (2014) *Gymnasiet som marknad,* Umeå: Boréa.
Maisuria, A. and Beach, D., (2017) Ethnography and education, *Oxford Research Encyclopedia of Education:* DOI: 10.1093/acrefore/9780190264093.013.100
Marx, K. and Engels, F., (1932) *The German ideology — critique of modern German philosophy according to its representatives Feuerbach, B. Bauer and Stirner, and of German socialism according to its various prophets:* https://www.marxists.org/archive/marx/works/1845/german-ideology/index.htm, accessed 1 December 2018
Massey, D., (1994/2013) *Space, place and gender,* Cambridge: Polity Press.
Neal, S., (2002) Rural landscapes, representations and racism: examining multicultural citizenship and policy-making in the English countryside, *Ethnic and Racial Studies,* 25(3): 442-461.
Nylund, M., (2012) The relevance of class in education policy and research: The case of Sweden's Vocational Education, *Education Inquiry,* 3(4): 591-613.
Öhrn, E., (2011) Class and ethnicity at work: segregation and conflict in a Swedish secondary school, *Education Inquiry,* 2(2): 345-355.
Öhrn, E., (2012a) Making a difference. Targets and resources for pupil influence, in T. Strand and M. Roos (eds.), *Education for social justice, equity and diversity* (pp. 19-36), Münster: LIT Verlag.
Öhrn, E., (2012b) Urban education and segregation: the responses from young people, *European Educational Research Journal,* 1(1): 45-57.
Öhrn, E. and Weiner, G., (2007) Urban education in Europe: section editors' introduction, in W. T. Pink and G. W. Noblit (eds.), *International handbook of urban education* (pp. 397-411), Dordrecht: Springer.
Raffo, C., (2011) Educational equity in poor urban contexts—exploring issues of place/space and young people's identity and agency, *British Journal of Educational Studies,* 59(1): 1-19.
Rosvall, P-Å. and Öhrn, E., (2014) Teachers' silences about racist attitudes and students' desires to address these attitudes, *Intercultural Education,* 25(5): 337-348.
Schwartz, A., (2013) *Pedagogik, plats och prestationer. En etnografisk studie om en skola i förorten.* [Pedagogy, place and performance: An ethnographic study about a school in a multicultural suburb: in Swedish with an English summary], Thesis, Gothenburg: Acta Universitatis Gothoburgensis.
Sernhede, O., (2007) Territorial stigmatisation. Hip Hop and informal schooling, in W. T. Pink and G. W. Noblit (eds.), *International handbook of urban education* (pp. 463-479), Dordrecht: Springer.
SOU, (2017) *Samling för skolan — Nationell strategi för kunskap och likvärdighet.* Swedish School Commission Report, 2017:35, Stockholm: Government Office.
Vaahtera, T., Niemi, A. M.., Lappalainen, S. and Beach, D., (2017) (eds.), *Troubling educational cultures in the Nordic countries,* London: Tufnell Press.
Vigo Arrazola, B. and Soriano Bozalongo, J., (2014) Teaching practices and teachers' perceptions of group creative practices in inclusive rural schools, *Ethnography and Education,* 9(2): 253-269.
Waara, P., (2011) Mellan något och någon—forskning om ungdom på landsbygden. [Between something and someone—research on youth in the countryside], in P. Möller (ed.), *Vem bygger landet?* Vilnius: Gidlunds förlag.
Young, I. M., (2001) Equality of whom? Social groups and judgements of injustice, *The Journal of Political Philosophy,* 9(1): 1-18.

Young, I. M., (2003) Political responsibility and structural justice, *The Lindley Lecture*, University of Kansas.
Young, I. M., (2004) Five faces of oppression, in L. Heldke and P. O'Conor (eds.), Oppression, privilege, and resistance: theoretical perspectives on racism, sexism, and heterosexism (pp. 37-63), New York: McGraw-Hill.

Ethnography and Education publications

Titles in the series include:

Creative learning: European experiences, edited by Bob Jeffrey;

Researching education policy: Ethnographic experiences, Geoff Troman, Bob Jeffrey and Dennis Beach;

Education and the commodity problem: Ethnographic investigations of creativity and performativity in Swedish schools. Dennis Beach and Marianne Dovemark;

Performing English with a postcolonial accent: Ethnographic narratives from Mexico, Angeles Clemente and Michael J. Higgins.

How to do Educational Ethnography, edited by Geoffrey Walford

Ritual and Identity; The staging and performing of rituals in the lives of young people, Christoph Wulf et al.

Young people's influence and democratic education: Ethnographic studies in upper secondary schools, edited by Elisabet Öhrn, Lisbeth Lundahl and Dennis Beach

Learner biographies and learning cultures: Identity and apprenticeship in England and Germany, Michaela Brockmann

Learning care lessons: Literacy, love, care and solidarity, by Maggie Feeley

Fair and competitive? Critical perspectives on contemporary Nordic schooling, editors, Anne-Lise Arnesen, Elina Lahelma, Lisbeth Lundahl and Elisabet Öhrn

Identity and social interaction in a multi-ethnic classroom, by Ruth Barley

The postmodern professional: Contemporary learning practices, dilemmas and perspectives, edited by Karen Borgnakke, Marianne Dovemark and Sofia Marques da Silva

Troubling educational cultures in the Nordic countries, edited by Touko Vaahtera, Anna-Maija Niemi, Sirpa Lappalainenand Dennis Beach

Arts and ethnography in a contemporary world: From learning to social participation, edited by Lígia Ferro and David Poveda

Further information available at

www.tufnellpress.co.uk

or

www.ethnographyandeducation.org

Milton Keynes UK
Ingram Content Group UK Ltd.
UKHW020756081023
430127UK00006B/27